SUSAN PRINCE TH

GEORGE THOMPSON

The Bhagavad Gītā

George Thompson, a Vedic scholar and Sanskritist, has more than twenty years of experience teaching the Bhagavad Gītā at college level. He is an assistant professor at Montserrat College of Art in Beverly, Massachusetts. He is currently preparing an anthology of translations from the Rigveda.

THE BHAGAVAD GITA

THE BHAGAVAD GITA

a new translation

George Thompson

NORTH POINT PRESS
A division of Farrar, Straus and Giroux
New York

NORTH POINT PRESS
A division of Farrar, Straus and Giroux
18 West 18th Street, New York 10011

Distributed in Canada by Douglas & McIntyre Ltd.
Printed in the United States of America
First edition, 2008

Library of Congress Cataloging-in-Publication Data
Bhagavadgita. English.
The Bhagavad Gita : a new translation / George Thompson. —1st ed.
p. cm.
Includes bibliographical references.
ISBN-13: 978-0-86547-744-5 (pbk. : alk. paper)
ISBN-10: 0-86547-744-2 (pbk. : alk. paper)
I. Thompson, George, 1951– II. Title.

BL1138.62.E5 2008
294.5'92404521—dc22

2008009010

Designed by Cassandra J. Pappas

www.fsgbooks.com

1 3 5 7 9 10 8 6 4 2

For

Susan, Akira, Nik, and Ruth,

and for

my entire kulaparamparā

ṛcó akṣáre paramé vyòman yásmin devā́ ádhi víśve niṣedúḥ |
yás tán ná véda kím ṛcā́ kariṣyati yá ít tád vidús tá imé sám āsate ||

—RIGVEDA 1.164.39,
THE RIDDLE HYMN ON "OM"

That syllable of the Rigveda, that highest space where all the gods have taken their places. What will he do with the Rigveda who does not know that syllable? Only those who know that sit together here with me!

Contents

A Note on This Translation

Charles Wilkins published the first translation of the Bhagavad Gītā into English in 1785, and there has been a steady stream of new translations ever since then. So inevitably a question arises that a translator of a new one must face: Why yet another version? This is my best attempt at an answer.

I have been teaching this text for many years, and I have used many of the available translations. There are quite a few reasonably reliable and accurate translations among them, but students have generally not responded well to the scholarly ones. I have no elaborate theory of translation, but because I am a philologist, I prefer an accurate translation to a loose one that may be more eloquent. Some eloquent translations of the Bhagavad Gītā have been made by people with little or no training in Sanskrit. Occasionally a student will ask me for permission to use one of them. I take such opportunities to compare translations, to show my students how different they can be. In this way, I emphasize the importance of choosing a translation that is accurate over one that may be easier to read or that appeals to a preconception that we might have of a given text, or religion, or culture. The popular literature that is readily available, not only in print but also increasingly online, concerning the traditions that I study and teach tends to conceal or ignore the little details that can make one tradition or text or passage distinctive, and therefore interesting.

I think it is necessary to try to present a text like the Bhagavad Gītā not only as accurately as possible, but also with a commitment to conveying its importance, both to those within its social and historical context—which in the case of the Bhagavad Gītā is very great indeed!—and to those whom we invite (or, in the case of students, require) to read it.

One of the reasons that I have taken up this translation is that I have long felt the need for one that is both accurate and engaging—and perhaps even eloquent. Over the years my students have complained that the verse translations of the Bhagavad Gītā were awkward, stiff, and sometimes hardly poetic at all. But my decision to make a vigorous, rhythmic prose translation is also rooted in my aim to make, first of all, an accurate translation. The Bhagavad Gītā is composed in a metrical form, mostly in a quatrain of eight-syllable lines known in Sanskrit as the *śloka*, or the *anuṣṭubh*. Occasionally the Bhagavad Gītā shifts into longer quatrains of four lines of eleven syllables, in interesting ways and at interesting times. But I think it has been a mistake to try to imitate or reproduce the quatrain stanzas in English.

The Bhagavad Gītā is a small section of that massive Sanskrit epic the Mahābhārata, the great encyclopedia of classical Indian culture. At its core, this encyclopedia is essentially an epic tradition; that is, it is fundamentally a narrative of war. The meter of Sanskrit epic poetry is not an elegant, finely tuned, finely crafted musical composition. In Sanskrit literature, such musical compositions were known as *kāvya*, a refined and complex genre of courtly poetry, intended for a highly educated elite audience. Sanskrit epic poetry, on the other hand, was governed by a loose and irregular meter, the primary function of which was simply to move the narrative along, quickly and easily. The Sanskrit of the epics, and of the Bhagavad Gītā, is much closer in fact to the colloquial everyday Sanskrit of the first century of the Common Era (C.E.). It is a vibrant and rhythmic kind of Sanskrit, much closer to what the spoken Sanskrit of the Brahmins and the warrior elite (*kṣatriya*s) must have sounded like at the time than to the earlier fundamentally esoteric poetry of the Rigveda, or to the later poetic language of Kālidāsa and the other courtly poets of classical India. Like the language of other epic poetries known to us, it is formulaic and improvisational. It is fast-paced and was readily accessible to its intended audience. What such an epic poetry needs in translation is a similarly colloquial, direct, and fast-paced English. That is what I have tried to produce in this translation.

To be sure, the Bhagavad Gītā does have highly poetic, even lyrical moments. It uses poetic figures more frequently than the Mahābhārata does as a whole, which is one reason why it is considered a later addition to the Mahābhārata. Nonetheless, the Bhagavad Gītā's poetic context, or rather its performance context, is much closer to the contemporary vernacular—that is, to ordinary speech—than to a high-register poetic language. And while the text undoubtedly contains many passages of genuine poetic brilliance and intensity, one also has to acknowledge that many passages in the Bhagavad Gītā are poetically very ordinary, and that a few are unconvertible, even by a great translator, into genuine poetry. Many of them come in the last six chapters, but even in the earlier chapters one sometimes encounters strange, awkward passages. One well-known example is Chapter 6, stanzas 5–7, where, in the course of two and a half brief *śloka*s, we encounter the word *ātman* no fewer than fifteen times. In stanza 6.5 alone—a mere thirty-two syllables in length—the word occurs seven times! I have spent a lot of time trying to work out how to translate this passage, and this is the best I could come up with:

5. One should lift one*self* up by means of the *self.* Do not degrade the *self,* for the *self* is one's only friend, and at the same time the *self* is one's only foe.
6. The self is one's friend when one has conquered the self by means of the self. But when a man neglects the self, then, like an enemy at war, that very self will turn against him.
7. A peaceful man who has mastered himself has a higher self that is deeply concentrated, whether in cold or in heat, whether in pleasure or in pain, whether in honor or in disgrace.

A more literal and more accurate translation of stanza 5 might be something like:

> One should lift up one*self* by means of the *self.* Do not degrade the *self,* for the *self* is one*self*'s only friend, and at the same time the *self* is one*self*'s only foe.

In this version, the seven occurrences of Sanskrit *ātman* in the stanza are represented by seven occurrences of *self* in the translation. There are other ways to translate this passage, but I have not found a way to make this passage genuinely "poetic" in English. Nor, as far as I know, has anyone else.*

There is also in fact another good reason to avoid translating the Bhagavad Gītā into versified quatrains. Traditionally, the Sanskrit epic text, including the Bhagavad Gītā, is presented in Sanskrit print editions in couplets (or pairs: hemistichs) of sixteen syllables

*In many passages, repetition is used for stylistic effect or to reinforce an idea. For example, at 1.12 the hero Bhīṣma is said to have "roared out a lion's roar." In the Sanskrit the noun for "lion's roar" is immediately followed by the verb "to roar." Likewise, 12.2 says "I consider them to be the best disciplined who focus their minds on me, who, constant in their discipline . . ." The repetition of "disciplined" and "discipline" reflects the emphatic repetition in the Sanskrit. A third example is 15.20, where the word "awakened" appears twice and will perhaps seem redundant to most readers. But once again the translation reflects the stylistic repetition of the Sanskrit.

each, because the basic semantic and syntactic unit of Sanskrit epic meter is really the couplet, not the quatrain. Sanskrit is fond of long compound words, as is readily apparent in the Bhagavad Gītā, with the often *very* long names of its heroic figures. Frequently, a quarter-stanza of eight syllables will consist of only one or two significant words—for example, a name accompanied by an epithet that is no more than metrical filler, or perhaps a verb accompanied by a preposition or an adverb—and also various emphatic particles that serve as mere metrical fillers as well. A more accurate imitation of the metrical form of the Bhagavad Gītā would consist of couplets of sixteen syllables each. Such a couplet would be roughly comparable to two lines of Homeric dactylic hexameter.

The standard Sanskrit *śloka* meter does not in general have the capacity to express complex abstract thought in a single stanza of thirty-two syllables. For this reason, the Bhagavad Gītā at times shifts to the longer *triṣṭubh* stanza of four lines of eleven syllables, thereby lengthening the individual stanza from thirty-two to forty-four syllables. We also frequently find single sentences extending across two or three or more stanzas, especially in those late chapters that present the popular Sāṁkhya philosophy of the time as long lists of qualities or features or habits that are characteristic of various types of people.

The Mahābhārata is a vast mosaic made up of huge and varied collections of smaller gems. While the size of these gems varies greatly, a significant number of them are roughly the same length as the Bhagavad Gītā, itself a "small classic" of seven hundred stanzas.* It is roughly as long as Greek and Roman dramas, and Sanskrit dramas as well. I would suggest that the Bhagavad Gītā, like other epic gems of similar size, was intended to be recited or sung in one session. It is

* For example, the famous episode of Nala and Damayantī, or the tale of Rāma, both in the third book, the Book of the Forest, of the Mahābhārata.

likely that in such sessions the performer would recite or sing from memory, or perhaps from a text. The audience, consisting of devotees of Kṛṣṇa, might accompany the performer, reciting favorite stanzas from memory, or perhaps listening silently in rapt meditation. In such a context, the recitation would have been rapid and rhythmic, emotional and devotional, rather than slow and pensive. My translation is intended to capture such a performance context.

On one matter I have decided to compromise literal accuracy for the sake of intelligibility, for a general non-Hindu audience. Throughout the Bhagavad Gītā, Arjuna and Kṛṣṇa address each other directly by name, but frequently their names are replaced by numerous popular epithets that are well known even today to an Indian audience. These epithets add nuance and texture to their personalities, and in the case of Kṛṣṇa also to the history of his assimilation to Viṣṇu (on which see "On the Organization of the Bhagavad Gītā," pp. xl–xliv). However, to a contemporary American audience, and especially to an inexperienced student audience, these epithets create a good amount of confusion. I have preferred for the most part neither to retain them nor to translate them at all, but rather to substitute the names of Arjuna and Kṛṣṇa as appropriate. The alternatives would have required too much explanatory apparatus, which would have distracted readers from the more important issues that the Bhagavad Gītā presents to us for our edification.

A Note on the Pronunciation of Sanskrit

In this edition, the transliteration of Sanskrit words into a Romanized alphabet with a set of standard conventional diacritical marks has been adopted, after a good amount of consideration of the alternatives. It would have been easier to adopt a more casual and informal system of transliteration. The name Krishna is now nearly universally recognized in the English-speaking world as the name of that most prominent Hindu god and the central figure of the Bhagavad Gītā. But in this translation, his name is always represented in the form *Kṛṣṇa*, which is how it is represented in the correct transcription of Sanskrit. Likewise, *Vishnu* is here rendered more accurately as *Viṣṇu*. The reason for this technical accuracy is not mere pedantry. All informal transcriptions run the risk of obscuring important distinctions in Sanskrit pronunciation. The most important example of this, because the most common, is the failure to distinguish between short and long vowels. If we ignore the long vowels in important names like Mahābhārata and Rāmāyaṇa, we will inevitably mispronounce them. In both instances, the accent falls on the last long vowel: thus *Mahābhā̲rata* and *Rāmā̲yaṇa* (where the syllable that receives the accent is underlined). We'll get back to accent in a moment.

The Sanskrit vowels should be pronounced as follows:

a	like	*u* in *cut* or the definite article *a*; Sanskrit example *mantra*
ā	like	*a* in *father*; Sanskrit example *ātman* or *jñāna*
i	like	*i* in *bit* or *sit*; Sanskrit example *Indra* or *nitya*
ī	like	*ee* in *meet*; Sanskrit example *gītā* or *īśvara*
u	like	*u* in *put*; Sanskrit example *buddhi* or *Buddha*
ū	like	*oo* in *boot*; Sanskrit example *bhūta* or *kūṭastha*
ṛ	like	*ri* in *risk* or *rig*; Sanskrit example *ṛta* or *ṛṣi* or *Kṛṣṇa*
ṝ	like	*ree* in *reel*; Sanskrit example *pitṝṇām* ("of the fathers")
e	like	*ay* in *say* or *pay*; Sanskrit example *tejas* or *namas te*
ai	like	*ai* in *aisle*; Sanskrit example *daiva* or *maitra*
o	like	*o* in *open*; Sanskrit example *loka* or *moha* or *OM*
au	like	*ou* in *sound*; Sanskrit example *Draupadī* or *Pauṇḍra*

The Sanskrit consonants are pronounced more or less as they are pronounced in English, except in the following instances:

c	like	*ch* in *church* (never like *c* in *cat*); Sanskrit example *cakra*

Sanskrit has a set of aspirated consonants: *kh, gh, ch, jh, ṭh, ḍh, th, dh, ph, bh.* These are pronounced like the corresponding nonaspirated consonants, *k, g, c, j, ṭ, ḍ, t, d, p, b,* with the addition of a heavy breathing. Thus, for example,

ph	like	*ph* in *shepherd* (never as in *photograph*); Sanskrit example *phala*

bh like *bh* in *clubhouse*; Sanskrit example *bhakti* or *Bhārata*

th like *th* in *boathouse* (never as in *think* or *bath*); Sanskrit example *atharva* or *ratha*

In the same way all of the other aspirated sounds of Sanskrit end with a breathy *h*.

Sanskrit also has a set of retroflex consonants (*ṭ, ṭh, ḍ, ḍh, ṇ, ṣ*) that are distinguished from the corresponding dental consonants (*t, th, d, dh, n, s*). The dentals are pronounced almost as in English, but with the tongue pressed against the teeth (as in Italian and other languages). The retroflex consonants are pronounced with the tongue curled back in the mouth. Some Sanskrit examples: *Kṛṣṇa, prāṇa, triṣṭubh, anuṣṭubh.* These retroflex sounds continue to be prominent in many Indian languages today, and can be easily recognized in contemporary Indian English as well.

Sanskrit has a set of six nasals (*ṅ, ñ, ṇ, n, m, ṁ*) and a set of three sibilants (*ś, ṣ, s*). Of these, the dental consonants *n, m,* and *s* are pronounced more or less as in English. The remaining nasals are pronounced:

ṅ like *ng* in *angle*; Sanskrit example *saṅga*

ñ like *ny* in *canyon*; Sanskrit *yajña* or *jñāna* (note that *jña* is frequently pronounced in India today with a hard *g*; thus *yajña* will often sound like *yagya* and *jñāna* like *gyāna*)

ṇ this is the retroflex nasal, as in *Kṛṣṇa, prāṇa, maṇḍala,* etc.

ṁ this is a sign of secondary nasalization before a consonant: thus *śaṁkara, sāṁkhya, saṁsāra, saṁnyāsin*

Of the three sibilants, *s* is pronounced as in English, *ś* is pronounced like *sh* in *shoe*, and *ṣ* is the retroflex sibilant, pronounced with the tongue curled back, as in *Kṛṣṇa*.

Finally, there is another secondary sign, *ḥ*, which is pronounced like *h* in English, but with a faint echo of the preceding vowel. Thus the famous mantra *om namaḥ śivāya*, where *namaḥ* will be heard as *namah*[a].

Back to the matter of long and short vowels, and how to pronounce the often very long names that we encounter in the Bhagavad Gītā. The rules for word accentuation in Sanskrit are very complicated, especially when it comes to the older language of the Vedas. Early Vedic Sanskrit had a variable pitch accent like Greek, but by the epic and classical period this pitch accent was lost and replaced by a stress accent that resembles the stress accent of Latin. The accentuation of Vedic words was variable also insofar as accent was sometimes placed on different syllables, or was even absent, depending on inflectional ending, sentence context, and so forth. Fortunately, we can ignore this extraordinary complexity when it comes to the Bhagavad Gītā and classical Sanskrit in general.

The basic rule for accent in classical and contemporary Sanskrit centers on the distinction between light and heavy syllables. Light syllables consist of a short vowel that is either followed by a single consonant or is itself isolated or final: thus the verb form *bhavati* has three light syllables and the accent is on the first. Heavy syllables may consist of a long vowel (*ā, ī, ū*) or a diphthong (*e, o, ai, au*) or a short vowel followed by more than one consonant.* Thus, in the

*Note that although the aspirated consonants mentioned above (*kh, gh, ch, jh, ṭh, ḍh, th, dh, ph, bh*) are represented by two consonants in standard Romanized transcription, they count in Sanskrit phonology, and in the script, as only a single consonant. Thus, in a word like *abhavat* ("became"), every syllable is light and every vowel is followed by only a single consonant. In Sanskrit phonology, *b* and *bh* both count as a single consonant with equal phonetic weight.

names Arjuna and Kṛṣṇa, the syllables *Arj* and *Kṛṣṇ* are both heavy, even though their vowels, the first *a* in *Arjuna* and *ṛ* in *Kṛṣṇa*, are both short. Since the syllable is heavy in both cases, it takes the accent. In general, the accent of a Sanskrit word falls on the next-to-last syllable if it is heavy (e.g., *ahaṁkāra*). If this syllable is light, then the accent falls on the third from the last syllable, again if it is heavy (e.g., *Mahābhārata* or *Rāmāyaṇa*). This is just as we find it in the pronunciation of Latin.

Sanskrit easily and frequently forms long compound words whose pronunciation will trouble the general reader uninitiated into its rhythms. But this conspicuous feature is not at all unique to Sanskrit. German is also fond of long compounds. Whereas we English speakers say "linguistics" or "the study of antiquity" (under the influence of Latin and French on English), German speakers say *"Sprachwissenschaft"* or *"Altertumswissenschaft."* This habit of compounding words without any helpful hyphens to guide us through them drove poor Mark Twain to write a very funny essay called "The Awful German Language," in which he complained (mock-) bitterly about such long word monstrosities as *Altertumswissenschaft.* Like German, Sanskrit will appear to the novice to be full of overly long words and names that are impossible to pronounce. But the pronunciation of the long Sanskrit names that we encounter in the Bhagavad Gītā and elsewhere in the vast world of Sanskrit literature is governed by the fairly simple rules that have been summarized above. Surprisingly quickly, one gets used to them, especially if one pays a little attention.

In a nutshell, one should pay close attention to the long and short vowels, as well as to the heavy and light syllables, because it is the long and heavy ones that tend to receive an accent, even when several of them appear in a single word. Thus, to return again to the names of the two great Sanskrit epics, the Mahābhārata and the Rāmāyaṇa, the main stress should be on the third syllable from the end in both words. But some stress should also be given to the other preceding long vowels as well. In fact, if you dwell a bit longer on all of the long vowels and heavy syllables of all Sanskrit words, while skipping lightly over all of the short vowels and light syllables, you will come off as a reasonably well-informed student of Sanskrit pronunciation.

Introduction

Some Observations on the Main Themes of the Bhagavad Gītā

Classical India knew and indeed cherished two large and immensely popular epic traditions, and we are fortunate that it preserved them both remarkably well, in the classical language of India, Sanskrit. These two epic cycles are the Mahābhārata and the Rāmāyaṇa. Both of them, but especially the Mahābhārata, grew over the course of many centuries to include and preserve a vast repertoire not only of epic (that is, warrior) legend, but also of mythological tales of gods and heroes, folk and fairy tales, love stories, proverbial wisdom literature and riddle tales, moral, philosophical, ritual, and finally religious discourses as well. The most prominent and well-known of all, both in India and beyond, is the small classic Bhagavad Gītā ("The Song of the Blessed One"), which forms part of the sixth book of the Mahābhārata. It has been one of the most important documents of traditional Hinduism ever since its composition, probably in the first century C.E.

Both the Mahābhārata and the Rāmāyaṇa begin with a core narrative that is quintessentially epic in theme. The Mahābhārata ("The

Great Tale of the Bhārata Clan") centers on a dynastic dispute between the five righteous Pāṇḍava brothers and their cousins, the Kauravas, which results in a gambling match. The five brothers lose the match, which leads to a very long period of exile for them and their wife in common, lasting for twelve years. They spend a thirteenth year hiding in the palace in disguise, in the kingdom of the Matsya clan. In the Rāmāyaṇa ("The Wanderings [or perhaps better, The Travels or Travails] of Rāma"), the unfailingly righteous Rāma is also exiled to the forest because of the imperial ambitions of a manipulative stepmother. Both epics contain the central message that our heroes must patiently endure the gross, flagrant injustices inflicted upon them, even by their own kin. In both epics they do so out of their unswerving commitment to *dharma*, "duty, righteousness, law." The focus on *dharma*, especially the *dharma* of the elite warrior caste, the Kṣatriyas, is the fundamental theme of both epics. It reflects the kind of stoicism and even fatalism that we typically find in the epic literature of a warrior elite. As a result, fate (Sanskrit *daiva*) is in fact an important theme in both of these epics.

Both epic cycles, as we have seen, were originally composed and performed orally, for the most part in a loosely rhythmical metrical stanza. Like other epics of world literature, the Sanskrit epics use a language that is highly formulaic, largely improvisational, and focused primarily on moving the story along quickly. The charioteer-bards,* who were well trained in these traditions, recited or perhaps sang these popular tales before audiences from the highest ranks of society, such as kings and the nobility, the Kṣatriyas, as well as high-caste Brahmin

*The Sanskrit word for charioteer-bard, both in the Bhagavad Gītā and in the epics in general, is *sūta*. Literally, the term means "charioteer," but since the charioteer also functioned as a bard, singing the praises of his heroic chariot-mate, the Sanskrit word refers to both functions. Note that the Bhagavad Gītā's frame narrator, Saṁjaya, is a *sūta*. So too is Kṛṣṇa. In the Mahābhārata, Kṛṣṇa is generally recognized as an adviser to the Pāṇḍavas. Only in the war episodes does he also take on the role of Arjuna's charioteer and bard. It is noteworthy that in the Mahābhārata Kṛṣṇa is a god in only a few special cases, like the Bhagavad Gītā.

priests. They performed these tales not only in Sanskrit, but eventually also in the vernacular languages of postclassical India, before the middle and lesser ranks of society as well. Often these audiences included even the lowest ranks, the low-caste villagers (*śūdra*s), for example, and women and children.* We know from the study of contemporary oral epic traditions, both in India and elsewhere, that the bards were free to emphasize, adorn, modify, add, or subtract certain elements of the story, as long as the story's core, which eventually became universally known to their audiences, was preserved unaltered (just as the Homeric tales, for example, came to be universally known to all Greeks of the classical period). Such easily generated and widely distributed variations were aimed at the given audience in attendance at a performance. For this reason, the repertoire of both story cycles grew to enormous proportions by the time they were eventually written down. The traditional text of the Rāmāyaṇa had grown to roughly 25,000 stanzas, while the traditional Mahābhārata grew to something like 100,000 stanzas in eighteen books, roughly eight times the length of the *Iliad* and the *Odyssey* combined.

It took many centuries, perhaps nearly a millennium, for these texts to reach such an enormous size. In fact, both epics were the collective enterprise of an entire culture. The Rāmāyaṇa is traditionally said to be the work of a single author called Vālmīki, while the Mahābhārata is attributed to Vyāsa. But the name of the latter is revealing: it means "the Arranger, the Compiler," which would suggest that he is more or less a mythical figure, like Homer among the Greeks, performing the function of the editor in the formation and growth of the tradition. It is generally estimated that the Sanskrit epics grew and flourished from roughly the fifth century B.C.E. to the

*See J.A.B. van Buitenen, *The Bhagavad Gītā in the Mahābhārata* (Chicago: University of Chicago Press, 1981), p. 10, where the commentator Bhāskara is quoted as asserting that *śūdras* and the like (that is, women) may listen only to the narrative parts of the epic, but not to the passages that present the esoteric teachings of the Vedānta, such as the Bhagavad Gītā.

fourth century C.E. As for the Bhagavad Gītā itself, a fairly short text of exactly seven hundred stanzas, scholars have debated whether it formed part of the original core of the Mahābhārata or was instead a later addition. And if it was *not* a part of that original core, then when, exactly, was it inserted into the great storehouse of the collective wisdom of India that the Mahābhārata has become? I tend to agree with those who argue for a relatively late date for the Bhagavad Gītā, perhaps somewhere in the first century C.E.*

At the time when the Sanskrit epics were formulated and collected, a great, formative cultural change took place in India: the emergence of a remarkably new kind of spirituality, from which the Bhagavad Gītā derives much of its inspiration. Around the second century B.C.E., expressions of an intense personal devotion to a particular deity began to emerge, with increasing passion. This new devotionalism, called *bhakti* in Sanskrit, was radically different from the traditional Vedic spirituality (dated roughly 1200 to 500 B.C.E.) that had preceded it by several centuries. Though reverence for the Vedic tradition, and especially for the Upaniṣads, continued to be expressed generally—at times in the Bhagavad Gītā itself—*bhakti* devotionalism was an explicit turning-away from the generally more impersonal sacrificial ritualism of the Vedas, which the high-caste Brahmins had preserved with great virtuosity, both in their memorization of the Vedic texts and in their performance of the Vedic rituals. The profoundly original spirituality of the Upaniṣads—that last creative phase of Vedic literature, which the Bhagavad Gītā frequently quotes with great favor—tended to be more impersonal, more philosophical, and more metaphysical than devotional. The Upaniṣads introduced many new concepts into the Brahmanical traditions that developed out of the older Vedas, and eventually they became one of the most

*See John Brockington, "The Sanskrit Epics," in Gavin Flood, ed., *The Blackwell Companion to Hinduism* (Oxford: Blackwell, 2003), pp. 116ff. For greater detail, see *The Sanskrit Epics* (Leiden: Brill, 1998).

important foundations of classical Hinduism, and a major source of inspiration for the Bhagavad Gītā. What the Bhagavad Gītā added to this Upaniṣadic tradition of meditation and yoga was its primary focus on the god Kṛṣṇa.

The Upaniṣads transformed the profoundly sacrificial tradition of the Vedas into a set of symbolic acts that no longer required the inherent violence of actual sacrifice, that is, the actual shedding of a sacrificial victim's blood. The famous opening passage of the Bṛhadāraṇyaka Upaniṣad catalogs in great detail the body parts of the Vedic sacrificial horse. Horse anatomy was well known to the Vedic clans because of the required ritual dismemberment, and the cataloging of the slain horse's body parts, in the Vedic horse sacrifice. The innovation that we see in this opening passage consists in equating the horse's body parts with significant parts of the cosmos. Thus the head of the horse is equated with the dawn, the horse's vision is the sun, its breath is the wind, its body is the year, the four limbs are the four seasons, its liver and lungs are the hills, and its body hairs are the plants and trees; when the horse urinates, it rains; and so forth.

In effect, this series of equations or identifications (in Sanskrit, called *bandhus*) achieves a symbolic or magical transformation of a violent act of animal sacrifice into a meditation on the reconstitution of the entire cosmos into all of its constituent parts. What we witness in this passage is a significantly new event: a Vedic teacher urging his students to understand that the age-old horse sacrifice, with all its violence and explicit obscenity (involving crude sexual taunting between high-caste Brahmin priests and the equally high-caste wives of the king), is not really a horse sacrifice at all! This kind of symbolic thinking, which is essentially magical,* came to be deeply influential

*The notion of magical thinking is controversial among Vedicists and scholars of religion in general, but it is not difficult to understand. In Joan Didion's book about her experience of the year following the sudden death of her husband, *The Year of Magical Thinking*, she describes her anguished, yearlong bout of magical thinking.

in Vedic culture and maintained a tenacious hold as well on post-Vedic culture—that is, classical Hinduism—for many centuries afterward. The Bhagavad Gītā ultimately rejects this kind of magical thinking, in favor of a newer religious sentiment. It advocates instead the devotee's personal surrender to the deity. The Bhagavad Gītā thereby solidified *bhakti* devotionalism as a major cultural force in classical India and centered it on the god Kṛṣṇa.

The authors of the Upaniṣads had also advocated an identification between the individual soul (the *ātman*) and the cosmic soul that pervades the universe (Brahman). This was a significant metaphysical step away from the magical equations of the sacrificial victim's body with the body of the cosmos that we see in the opening passage of the Bṛhadāraṇyaka Upaniṣad.* This advance in philosophical sophistication is illustrated by another famous passage, again from the early Upaniṣads: stanza 6.3 of the Chāndogya Upaniṣad, where the individual soul or self (the *ātman*) is ultimately equated with the infinite cosmic self (Brahman). Clearly, this Vedic equation took deep roots in the Bhagavad Gītā as well, where Kṛṣṇa frequently identifies himself with this infinite Brahman. (See examples in Chapters 5, 6, and 8, among many others.) In the Bhagavad Gītā, the *ātman* is eternal, and is ultimately unaffected by events in the natural world (*prakṛti*) and its three qualities (*guṇas*). This conception of the *ātman* is extremely important in the Bhagavad Gītā, which refers to this utterly spiritual, nonmaterial entity—the individual soul—by means of many other Sanskrit terms: for example, *dehin*, "the embodied one"; or *puruṣa*, "the person, spirit"; or *kṣetrajña*, "the knower of the field." Less frequent but equally revealing are terms like *sākṣin*, "the witness," and *udāsīna*, "the impartial bystander" or "the reliable

*This sort of equation has a long history in Vedic going all the way back to the famous *Puruṣa-sūkta* (Hymn to the Primordial Man) of the Rigveda, at 10.90. In this hymn the gods sacrifice and dismember this first sacrificial victim, thus bringing about the creation of this world.

witness." All these terms are used to describe the ultimate detachment of the *ātman* from the inevitable troubles of this world.

Another feature of the philosophy of the Bhagavad Gītā that deserves attention is the fact that reincarnation is so well entrenched in it that it is simply taken for granted. The doctrine of the perpetual reincarnation of the *ātman* goes back, once again, to the Upaniṣads. In this view, the *ātman* is born, and dies, and is reborn again—and again and again—in a long string of lives that does not end until the individual realizes his or her identity with infinite Brahman. While the Bhagavad Gītā is not the source of this doctrine, it is a very successful popularization—perhaps one of the most successful popularizations—of this doctrine in all of Hindu literature. Notably, both Buddhism and Jainism, which reject so many core doctrines of the Hindu traditions, readily accept the doctrine of reincarnation. They both also embrace its corollary, the doctrine of karma: the view, that is, that one's actions have inevitable consequences, not only in this life, but in all the lives that follow it. The notions of karma and reincarnation are deeply embedded and pervasive in Indian culture; it is hard to imagine an India that did not have these ideas as central elements in its worldview.

As we have seen, many crucial Upaniṣadic ideas endured well beyond the Vedic period, which essentially came to an end with the advent of the many heterodox and profoundly ascetic traditions, especially Buddhism and Jainism, in about the fourth century B.C.E. Clear traces of asceticism had already appeared within the Vedic tradition as well, which, especially in the Upaniṣads, put great new emphasis on the personal liberation (Sanskrit *mokṣa*, and in Buddhism, *nirvāṇa*) of the individual from all social (and especially caste) obligations. In Sanskrit these were called *śramaṇa* traditions, that is, the traditions of those who renounce the world. By rejecting the spiritual authority of the Vedic tradition, Buddhism, Jainism, and similar movements offered themselves as alternatives to the caste system, with its elaborate network of restrictive and rigid—and at times brutally oppressive—social obligations. Buddhism, Jainism, and the other *śramaṇa* traditions refocused spirituality away from social obligations (i.e., caste *dharma*) and trained it instead on the individual's deliverance from suffering. This shift is clearly illustrated by the Four Noble Truths of Buddhism, which assert that all life is suffering, that the cause of suffering is desire, that suffering can be extinguished, and that the eightfold path of Buddhism is the means to extinguishing it. In Buddhism the term *dharma* takes on this new, less socialized meaning. The emphasis on personal liberation is also reflected in Jainism's adamant focus on complete nonviolence (Sanskrit *ahiṁsā*), an enormous influence on Gandhi. These traditions emphasized withdrawal from a social system about which they tended to be very pessimistic, even contemptuous at times, and triggered a turn in classical India toward monasticism and asceticism.

Although the Bhagavad Gītā never directly refers to these ascetic *śramaṇa* traditions, it can nevertheless be seen as a response to the challenge that these movements posed to traditional Brahmanic Hinduism. But its counterargument against them is a remarkably unexpected one. The Bhagavad Gītā at times does gesture toward a philosophy of nonviolence—the word *ahiṁsā* occurs in the Bhagavad Gītā four times—but *never* as a central tenet of its teaching. The word always occurs in lists of the virtues—of the wise man, or the "knower of the field," or the man born into divine circumstance, or finally the man who possesses the quality, the disposition, of clarity (*sāttvika*). But by and large the Bhagavad Gītā is a kind of counterintuitive challenge to the conventional morality of those who would preach nonviolence. Kṛṣṇa's ultimate goal is to persuade Arjuna to pick up his weapons and fight. Implicit in the view of the Bhagavad Gītā, as in the Mahābhārata as a whole, is the belief that in this world violence, like action itself, is inevitable.

As the Bhagavad Gītā opens, Arjuna is expressing moral qualms against this war between cousins. He looks across the battlefield at both of the assembled armies. He sees kinsmen on both sides, revered teachers and dear cousins and cherished childhood playmates. This arouses a moral reaction in him that we all can recognize as true and right. His moral sense tells Arjuna clearly that such a war, especially among kin, is utterly wrong. It is clear that his qualms against this impending doomsday battle are impeccably moral, and as such should be highly commendable. Who among us would not want to see such moral qualms expressed, and acted upon, today? But paradoxically Kṛṣṇa does not commend Arjuna's moment of conscience. Instead he dismisses it as weakness of nerve, unfitting in a nobleman. Any warrior or soldier anywhere will be familiar with this sort of response. It appeals to the sense of shame that soldiers feel before their peers at experiencing a failure of nerve at some moment of crisis on the battlefield. This argument from shame is a well-worn cliché of epic literature and is frequently expressed throughout our two Sanskrit epic cycles. But as a cliché, it does not move Arjuna to change his mind. Arjuna shows that he is a truly moral agent, and not just a coward, as Kṛṣṇa at first seems to suggest.

Thereafter Kṛṣṇa presents an argument to Arjuna that dismisses what might be called traditional ethics, at least from a Western, or perhaps a secular or worldly, point of view. But from Kṛṣṇa's point of view—the point of view of eternity—Arjuna's moral stance is immature. It is a myopic view of the world that is driven, simply and crudely, by desire, and it makes no difference that the desire is for peace rather than for war. Kṛṣṇa's answer to Arjuna's moral qualms comes down to this: In the long run, inevitably, we all must die. Since death is inevitable, there is no point in lamenting it. We must do the right thing, *dharma*, no matter what that might entail. If the fulfillment of *dharma* requires the execution of cousins, teachers, and friends, well then, so be it. When the message is put this bluntly, it seems harsh indeed.

Consider the following stanzas from Chapter 2:

11. You grieve for those who are beyond grieving, and you talk like one with wisdom, but the truly learned grieve neither for those who have lost their lives nor for those who still have them.
12. But in fact there never was a time when I did not exist, nor you, nor any of these other lords. And there never will be a time when we do not exist.
13. Just as the embodied one experiences childhood, and youth, and old age, in this body, in the same way he enters other bodies. A wise man is not disturbed by this.
14. O Arjuna, encounters with the material world induce sensations of cold and heat and pleasure and pain. They come and they go. They are impermanent. You are a Bhārata! Endure them!

Kṛṣṇa's words concerning the impermanence of human life have appeared to many readers to actually devalue life, which, though transitory, is nevertheless precious to most of us. The implications of his view (one of which is to justify war) have long troubled many readers as well. At 11.32, Kṛṣṇa famously says:

> I am time, the agent of the world's destruction, now grown old and set in motion to destroy the worlds. Even without you, all of these warriors arrayed in opposing battle-formation will cease to exist!

These words (and in fact all of Chapter 11, where Kṛṣṇa reveals himself as the god of all things) are frequently met with shock or dismay among Western readers unfamiliar with Hindu traditions. They frequently think this stanza is the expression of an almost nihilistic indifference to human suffering and to the perpetual problem of war and violence. But in fact these words and the whole chapter are a profound meditation not on war but on time (Sanskrit *kāla*), which, like the Vedic god of fire, Agni, consumes all things. The image of time as a huge gaping mouth in which we are all consumed in a blaze of fire is an old and venerable one in India, dating all the way back to the oldest of the Vedas.

But I think that one encounters a certain terror in the face of time wherever time is examined closely. Saint Augustine, for example, offers profound speculations on the psychology of time, in his exquisite Latin prose, in the *Confessions*: "What, then, is time? If no one asks me, surely, I know; if I want to explain it to someone who does ask me, however, I do not know." (*Quid est ergo tempus? si nemo ex me quaerat, scio; si quaerenti explicare velim, nescio.*—*Confessions* 11.14) And later, he writes: "My mind is on fire to know this most intricate of riddles." (*Exarsit animus meus nosse istuc inplicatissimum aenigma.*—*Confessions* 11.22) Or consider the astonishing, brooding final sentence of Claude Lévi-Strauss's *The Naked Man* (volume 4 of his *Introduction to a Science of Mythology*). The sentence goes on for twenty-two lines, or well over two hundred words, and concludes with these: "[At some future point in time man's] sorrows, his joys, his hopes and his works will be as if they had never existed, since no consciousness will survive to preserve even the memory of these ephemeral phenomena, only a few features of which, soon to be erased from the impassive face of the earth, will remain as already cancelled evidence that they once were, and were as nothing."

Here Lévi-Strauss is clearly contemplating a nuclear holocaust, which these days at times appears to be hurtling toward us at frightening speed. The vision of what will remain after such a holocaust calls to mind the words of J. Robert Oppenheimer, the celebrated "father of the nuclear bomb" and a brilliant polymath who had studied Sanskrit and Eastern philosophy while a student at Harvard. The philosophy of the Bhagavad Gītā had had a profound effect on him, he told us, and on several occasions, when asked what thoughts had crossed his mind while witnessing the first atomic explosion, he chose to quote two passages from Chapter 11 of the Bhagavad Gītā:

> 12. If the light of a thousand suns were to suddenly arise in heaven—as at the dawn of a new age—that would be like the radiance of this great soul!

And then a stanza already quoted above:

> 32. I am time, the agent of the world's destruction, now grown old and set in motion to destroy the worlds. Even without you, all of these warriors arrayed in opposing battle-formation will cease to exist!*

These stanzas are much quoted in the literature on nuclear weapons, and are well known to students and even to schoolchildren. They reflect Oppenheimer's awe and deep ambivalence about what he had helped to create, and then witnessed, in that desolate New Mexican desert in the 1940s. Lévi-Strauss's philosophical reflections, at the end of his lifelong project to understand the workings of the human mind, begin with what Lévi-Strauss refers to as Hamlet's dilemma: that "man is not free to choose whether to be or not to be." Awareness of time, the inevitable passing of human time—that little bit of human light between two immense, dark eternities—is, according to Lévi-Strauss, at the heart of *all* human experience. The author

*Oppenheimer used the 1944 translation by Swami Nikhilananda, which renders these passages in this way: "If the radiance of a thousand suns were to burst into the sky, that would be like the splendour of the Mighty One" (11.12); and "Now I am become Death, the destroyer of worlds . . ." (11.32, only in part).

of the Bhagavad Gītā—like the authors of the Homeric epics and of Gilgamesh, like the Romantic poets Keats and Wordsworth and Shelley, and more recently the American Transcendentalists Whitman, Emerson, and Thoreau, only a few examples among countless others—all know deeply this truth about time and its terrors.

In India, however, and in the Bhagavad Gītā, time is cyclical and thus unending, but also therefore dreadfully repetitive. A well-known aphorism from the Mahābhārata goes something like this: "Brahma said, 'Well, after hearing ten thousand explanations, a fool is no wiser, But an intelligent man needs only two thousand five hundred.' "* In a few words, this charming and amusing aphorism (of which there are many in the Mahābhārata) illustrates "the long view" of time that is adopted widely in India and, in the Bhagavad Gītā, by "that man who stands on the mountaintop" (Sanskrit *kūṭastha*), alone, aloof, abiding in eternal Brahman. This long view of time can be maintained, it seems, without renouncing a good sense of humor.

The central figure of the Bhagavad Gītā is Kṛṣṇa, "the Blessed One" (the Sanskrit term is *bhagavant*, from which the form *bhagavad* of the Gītā's title is derived). With a few important exceptions, the Bhagavad Gītā is largely a monologue in which Kṛṣṇa not only urges Arjuna to resume his duty as a warrior but, much more important, introduces Arjuna to a truer, higher, reality: Kṛṣṇa himself as he really is. In much of the rest of the Mahābhārata Kṛṣṇa is portrayed simply as a human being, Arjuna's companion and charioteer. But in the Bhagavad Gītā Kṛṣṇa becomes the central figure, the central reality, and Arjuna comes to realize that he has been behaving rather too casually toward his so-called charioteer. In Chapter 11, where Arjuna describes the great theophany of Kṛṣṇa, which no one before him had been able to see, Arjuna's relationship with Kṛṣṇa takes a

*William Buck, *Mahabharata Retold* (Berkeley and Los Angeles: University of California Press, 1973), p. 71.

dramatic turn. Kṛṣṇa is no longer Arjuna's companion; no, he is Arjuna's god. At 11.39–40, Arjuna is scarcely able to say much at all to Kṛṣṇa beyond stammering "Homage, homage" repeatedly. This Sanskrit form of address, *namas*, which is more like a gesture of obeisance, occurs no fewer than six times here:

> Homage to you, a thousand homages to you! And again homage to you!
>
> Homage before you and homage behind you, let there be homage to you, the all, on all sides!

And immediately after, at 11.41–42, Arjuna apologizes profusely to Kṛṣṇa:

> Whatever I may have said impulsively, thinking "This is my friend," addressing you "Hello Kṛṣṇa, hello Yādava, hello my friend!" unaware as I was of your true greatness, whether out of carelessness or affection,
>
> and if while joking I have said something offensive, while relaxing or resting or sitting or eating with you—whether alone or publicly—immeasurable Kṛṣṇa, I seek your forgiveness.

At this point Arjuna is the subordinate companion. In fact, he has become Kṛṣṇa's prostrate devotee. And Kṛṣṇa has become Arjuna's awesome and terrible god and teacher.

In this role, Kṛṣṇa introduces Arjuna to the new devotionalism. Two important features of the new spirituality should be mentioned: the traditional school of Hindu philosophy, Sāṁkhya, and another that is closely associated with it, yoga. Besides being a song of devotion to Kṛṣṇa, the Bhagavad Gītā is also a somewhat unsystematic synthesis of many popular and influential contemporary schools of thought. The Sāṁkhya school is basically a naturalistic, nontheistic philosophy. The term *sāṁkhya* literally means "enumeration, classification." Its primary focus is on characterizing and classifying cosmological and psychological processes, the processes of the natural world (*prakṛti*). It examines the network of interactions of the three "qualities" (*guṇas*) of nature. Cosmologically, these *guṇas* refer to the conditions of nature. They are *sattva* (clarity, integrity, purity), *rajas* (passion or energy), and *tamas* (darkness or inertia). All of the things of nature consist of these three qualities in varying measure. Psychologically, they refer to a person's natural tendencies or inclinations, to mental dispositions. Thus one who is inclined toward a *sāttvic* (Sanskrit *sāttvika*) temperament will display the virtues of clarity, integrity, and purity; one inclined toward a *rājasic* (Sanskrit *rājasa*) temperament will display great energy and passion; on the other hand, one who is inclined toward a *tāmasic* (Sanskrit *tāmasa*) temperament will wallow in laziness, sluggishness, and inertia. There is also a fundamental dualism in Sāṁkhya, a division between nature (*prakṛti*) and spirit (*puruṣa*). The Bhagavad Gītā makes use of this dualism in its characterizations of the relationship between the individual soul (*ātman*), which is ultimately identical with Brahman, and the material world, which is not. In the process, the Bhagavad Gītā modifies Sāṁkhya thought so that it too reflects a more fundamental driving force: the Bhagavad Gītā's theistic, devotional focus on Kṛṣṇa.

The last six chapters of the Bhagavad Gītā tend to be far less poetical or religious or philosophical, and far more formulaic and mechanical, than the earlier chapters. They summarize the traditional Sāṁkhya doctrine that was popular at the time and tend conspicuously toward a style of Sanskrit—the *sūtra* style—that, although composed in verse, tends to be terse, even to the point of lapsing into simple lists and catalogs. The Bhagavad Gītā's overview of the Sāṁkhya school of philosophy is fairly faithful to the spirit of Sāṁkhya as we find it in its later classical form. But this summary does not seem integral to the overall aim of the Bhagavad Gītā, which is profoundly theistic and adamantly devotional, ultimately focused on Kṛṣṇa. Elsewhere in the Bhagavad Gītā, the primary focus of discussion is always on Kṛṣṇa and always culminates in Kṛṣṇa. In these later chapters, however, Kṛṣṇa is more or less absent, and relatively little reference to him is made until the final concluding sections, which attempt to tie the pieces of the Bhagavad Gītā together.

Yoga, on the other hand, is an utterly central notion in the Bhagavad Gītā from beginning to end. It is considered to be a traditional school of philosophy largely because of its association with the more theoretical and classifying Sāṁkhya school. Nevertheless, as a practical spiritual discipline, yoga is as fundamental to the philosophy of the Bhagavad Gītā as Kṛṣṇa himself is. Yoga is, after all, the vehicle by means of which one attains to Kṛṣṇa, by means of which one truly comes to know him. Through yoga one gains true knowledge of the self, or the *ātman*, which is ultimately not engaged in the perpetual turmoil of time and the natural world. Yoga is the vehicle by means of which one accomplishes renunciation (*saṁnyāsa*) and the abandonment (*tyāga*) of the fruits of one's actions. In the Bhagavad Gītā, the word *yoga* occurs roughly 150 times—far, far more often than any of its other key terms. Clearly, yoga is in the Bhagavad Gītā the most basic tool of spiritual development.

Besides introducing a hierarchical classification of the types of yoga (*karmayoga*, "the yoga of action"; *jñānayoga*, "the yoga of knowledge"; *bhaktiyoga*, "the yoga of devotion"), the Bhagavad Gītā offers yoga as a resource to everyone, no matter what their caste or station. Remarkably, the Bhagavad Gītā asserts that the yoga of devotion, *bhakti*, is the best yoga, because it is the most accessible form of yoga—available to as many people as possible. This gesture toward even the lowest castes makes the Bhagavad Gītā a very desirable alternative, for Hindus of all castes, to the anticaste spirit of the heterodox traditions like Buddhism and Jainism, which in fact had made great headway against Brahmanical, caste-conscious Hinduism before the Bhagavad Gītā itself was composed.

Within its historical social context, the Bhagavad Gītā successfully defended traditional Hinduism against the incursions of anticaste traditions like Buddhism and Jainism by offering yoga to absolutely everyone. Made available to one and all, yoga enabled an individual to cultivate a detached state of mind under any and all circumstances. It equipped the individual to perform the obligatory duties that inevitably called him away from his own individual liberation. Traditionally, all Hindus, following in the footsteps of the high-caste Brahmins, are obliged to pass through four stages of life, without skipping any of them: that of the celibate student (*brahmacārya*); that of the householder (*gṛhastha*), who makes a family and also the money to support it; that of the hermit or forest-dweller (*vanaprastha*), who, having provided well for his family, can now say goodbye to it with a good conscience; and finally, that of the renouncer or renunciate (*saṁnyāsin*), who is ready to prepare himself seriously for the final reality. To abandon any one of these life-stages prematurely, without regard either for one's ancestors or for one's future progeny, in order to selfishly secure one's own liberation, as Buddhism and Jainism urge, was generally viewed as unacceptable within traditional Brahminical society.

Thus the Bhagavad Gītā effectively resolved the tension between two opposed sets of values. It preserved the caste-oriented social institutions that held the culture together and, at the same time, allowed an individual to seek salvation outside of them. This was a brilliant and effective resolution of an enduring tension between the aims of the individual and the obligations and sacrifices required by a rigid caste-governed society. This was one of the Bhagavad Gītā's greatest and most enduring achievements and is a reason that it continues to have great appeal to people in so many other cultures even now. Along with the *Yoga Sūtras* of Patañjali, the Bhagavad Gītā is a major source of insight into the contemporary practice of yoga all over the world.

On the Organization of the Bhagavad Gītā

Chapter 1 begins with a catalog of names, just like the catalog of ships in the *Iliad.* In epic traditions it was obligatory to list the names of the heroes and heroic families who participated in epic wars. The singer of epic tales almost everywhere, it seems, was obliged to name the significant figures who participated in the war that the epic celebrated. Such catalogs will no doubt seem tedious to most readers, removed as we now are from the original historical events that inspired them. But we should try to understand the purpose of these catalogs. They confirm that a specific hero or clan participated in a given historic war, and they assert that this participation should be remembered. This is not very different from the Vietnam War Memorial in Washington, D.C., which lists the names of all of the U.S. soldiers who died in the Vietnam War. Though we are separated by more than two thousand years from the events described in the Bhagavad Gītā, we nevertheless know the names of the most significant actors on the battlefield of Kurukṣetra. This would no doubt please the author of the Bhagavad Gītā and his aristocratic patrons, who took the trouble to preserve the names of the heroes of this family tradition from the beginning of Indian history. That we are still seeing their names, not only in India but everywhere the Bhagavad Gītā continues to be read, is a measure of the continuing success of its author. And whoever he was (tradition knows him as Vyāsa), he knew what he was doing and was very good at doing it. In terms of genre, the Bhagavad Gītā is not only an enormously influential religious song (*gītā*). It is also a fine piece of epic poetry.

The author of the Bhagavad Gītā impersonates Kṛṣṇa throughout much of the text. This author is in fact anonymous, since Vyāsa is simply a traditional name for anyone who has contributed to the collected wisdom of the Mahābhārata. It may be helpful to take a closer look at what this anonymous poet-bard is up to in the Bhagavad Gītā.

The basic dialogue form of the Bhagavad Gītā is framed by the external narration of Saṁjaya, a bard and charioteer (like Kṛṣṇa himself throughout much of the Mahābhārata), who narrates to the blind king Dhṛtarāṣṭra what he observes taking place on the battlefield. Because he has received a "divine eye" from Vyāsa, Saṁjaya can see things taking place at great distances, and he can magically hear all of the intimate details of the long conversation between Arjuna and Kṛṣṇa, as they stand on the battlefield of Kurukṣetra, the field of the Kurus. Saṁjaya thus functions as the Bhagavad Gītā's "omniscient narrator."

Beyond this omniscient narrator, Saṁjaya, who occasionally intercedes to set the scene, the Bhagavad Gītā is basically a dialogue between Arjuna and his charioteer-bard (*sūta*), Kṛṣṇa. However, given that Kṛṣṇa is the supreme god of the Bhagavad Gītā, we could say that the author of the Bhagavad Gītā basically plays two roles: when he speaks in the role of Arjuna, he impersonates Arjuna, and when he speaks in the role of Kṛṣṇa, he impersonates Kṛṣṇa.

Although it does not use the term *avatāra* (Sanskrit *avatāra* literally means "descent"), the Bhagavad Gītā implicitly recognizes the *avatāra* doctrine, the view that Viṣṇu descends to earth at various times to be embodied in a number of incarnations. Thus Viṣṇu is traditionally recognized to have descended and made himself manifest in such forms as a fish (Matsya) and a tortoise (Kūrma) and a wild boar (Varāha). He also took on human forms such as a dwarf (Vāmana) and a man-lion figure (Nṛsiṁha). Other traditionally well-known figures were considered to be avatars of Viṣṇu as well: Vyāsa, the compiler, himself was considered to be one of Viṣṇu's avatars, as were Rāma of epic tradition, the Buddha, and Kṛṣṇa.*

In the development of classical Hindu tradition, three gods came

*The presence of the Buddha in this list of Viṣṇu's avatars may surprise some readers. But the *avatāra* doctrine was a method of assimilating new religious movements, as they arose, into the tradition of Viṣṇu, thus making them a part of an endlessly unfolding Vaiṣṇava tradition. There are many traditional lists of Viṣṇu's avatars of varying length. For a detailed summary, see A. Danielou, *Hindu Polytheism* (New York: Pantheon, 1969).

to stand out from the rest. These three are Brahmā, Viṣṇu, and Śiva. Together they form what in Sanskrit is called the Trimūrti, the three supreme forms of God. Conventionally, Brahmā is characterized as "the Creator," Viṣṇu as "the Preserver," and Śiva as "the Destroyer." At the time when the Bhagavad Gītā was composed, all three of these gods were already widely worshipped throughout India. But not one of them is mentioned frequently in the Bhagavad Gītā. Kṛṣṇa would eventually become one of the great avatars of Viṣṇu, like the hero Rāma of the Rāmāyaṇa. That the Bhagavad Gītā is familiar with the *avatāra* doctrine is evident from the fact that it alludes to it, without using the term *avatāra*, at 4.7–8, where Kṛṣṇa says:

> Whenever religious duty [*dharma*] wanes, Arjuna, and its opposite, chaos [*adharma*], waxes strong, then I release myself into the world.
>
> In age after age, I manifest myself in order to protect the virtuous, to destroy those who do harm, and to reestablish religious duty.

But the name Viṣṇu is explicitly applied to Kṛṣṇa only three times in the Bhagavad Gītā: once at 10.21, where Kṛṣṇa says that among the divine sons of Aditi he is Viṣṇu, and twice in Chapter 11, where Arjuna addresses Kṛṣṇa directly as Viṣṇu (11.24 and 11.30). Elsewhere in the Bhagavad Gītā, Kṛṣṇa is occasionally referred to by epithets that are also used to refer to Viṣṇu in other parts of the Mahābhārata (as well as in other texts), but it is a striking fact—which needs to be explained—that in the Bhagavad Gītā, Kṛṣṇa refers to himself as Viṣṇu *only* once (at 10.21), and that Arjuna refers to Kṛṣṇa as Viṣṇu *only* twice, and in both instances in that strangely anomalous and possibly later Chapter 11, where Kṛṣṇa reveals himself as he really is to Arjuna. In fact, Chapter 11 appears to be an insertion, a short Arjuna

Gītā within the Bhagavad Gītā. All this suggests that the identification of Kṛṣṇa as an avatar of Viṣṇu was not yet settled doctrine at the time of the Bhagavad Gītā. Such an identification seems to have been an innovation initiated by the Bhagavad Gītā itself.

The notion of an infinite cosmological god, Brahman, that dwells within each individual soul, or *ātman*, at its core and that is ultimately equivalent with all things is firmly rooted in and fundamental to the Bhagavad Gītā. Insofar as each of us is an *ātman*, we are all ultimately identical with this infinite Brahman as well. But in the Bhagavad Gītā this infinite Brahman is always referred to as a neuter noun, *brahman*, and therefore distinct from a masculine god, Brahmā. The masculine name of this infinite god appears twice, both times in Chapter 11 (11.15 and 11.37). At 11.15 Arjuna sees Brahmā sitting on his lotus seat surrounded by all the gods, but he sees them all as dwelling within Kṛṣṇa's body! And at 11.37 Arjuna tells Kṛṣṇa:

> And why shouldn't they pay homage to you, great soul—a creator more worthy than Brahmā himself? You are the infinite lord of the gods and the world's resting place. You are the imperishable, both what exists and what does not exist, and beyond them both.

Finally, there is no direct mention of Śiva in the Bhagavad Gītā, but an allusion to Śiva seems to occur at 10.23, where Kṛṣṇa says, "Among the terrifying deities I am the gentle one [that is, Śiva]." This is just two stanzas after the stanza where Kṛṣṇa identifies himself as Viṣṇu, as well as the entire pantheon of gods who are all present at Kṛṣṇa's great theophany.

One of the ambitions of the author of the Bhagavad Gītā was clearly to establish Kṛṣṇa as the supreme deity. Nowhere is such an ambition clearer than in the very important Chapter 11. But the basic means that he used to accomplish his goal was to emphatically identify Kṛṣṇa, not with any one of these three supreme gods, not even with Viṣṇu, but instead with the neutral, impassive, infinite Brahman. Eventually, the Bhagavad Gītā came to be identified as a Vaiṣṇava text, that is, a text embraced by those traditions that worship Viṣṇu. But in its origins, the Bhagavad Gītā appears to have been far more focused on Kṛṣṇa himself.

For anyone who wishes to come to an understanding of and a feeling for classical India, and for India today as well, the Bhagavad Gītā is a crucial source. Many of the most fundamental ideas that animate Indian cultural life can be found vividly displayed within this dialogue that we are permitted to listen in on, in spite of the thunderous din of conch shells being blown on all sides. Kṛṣṇa's appeal to Arjuna to embrace his duty as a warrior, to commit himself to action while renouncing any and all consequences, and to convert all of his actions into a sacrifice offered to Kṛṣṇa himself has fascinated countless devotees of Kṛṣṇa ever since.

A Note on Chapter 11

Chapter 11, the great epiphany—theophany, really—where Kṛṣṇa compassionately condescends to reveal his true nature to Arjuna, has a significant metrical shift that has led some scholars to think that it might be an autonomous portion of the Bhagavad Gītā. Although the Bhagavad Gītā occasionally slides into the longer *triṣṭubh* stanza (which consists of four lines of eleven syllables) instead of the Bhagavad Gītā's standard *śloka* stanza (which consists of four lines of eight syllables), this metrical shift is most conspicuous and most dramatic in Chapter 11, long stretches of which are composed in this longer stanza.

The astonishing, ineffable things that Arjuna sees when Kṛṣṇa gives him a "divine eye," so that he can see Kṛṣṇa as he really is (recall Saṁjaya's divine eye, so that Saṁjaya can also see and hear all that is taking place on that remote battlefield), are described by Arjuna rather than by Kṛṣṇa himself. In other words, Chapter 11 is composed from Arjuna's perspective, not from Kṛṣṇa's. As such, it is in effect an Arjuna Gītā rather than a Bhagavad Gītā, that is, a short soliloquy by Arjuna embedded within a much larger discourse from Kṛṣṇa, the Bhagavad Gītā as a whole.

This view of Chapter 11 as an interpolation has been argued by a number of scholars, but I think that a much stronger case can be made, and perhaps this introduction is a good place to make it. In the immediately preceding chapter, Chapter 10, Kṛṣṇa recites his powers, or manifestations (Sanskrit *vibhūti*s). Except for seven early stanzas (10.12–18) where Arjuna asks Kṛṣṇa to talk about these powers, the entire chapter of forty-two stanzas belongs to Kṛṣṇa alone. To a great extent, what Kṛṣṇa says in Chapter 10 consists of a series of statements of the type "Among X, I am Y." For example:

> 21. Among the divine sons of Aditi I am Viṣṇu. Among the celestial lights I am the radiant sun. I am lightning among the gods of the storm. And I am the moon among the stars.
> 22. Among the Vedas I am the Sāmaveda, the book of songs. Among the gods I am Indra, their king. Among the senses I am the mind, and among the sentient I am consciousness.

These sets of "I am . . ." assertions fill up the vast majority of this chapter, and they are what I call, after the Sanskrit term *ātmastuti*, assertions of self-praise. In such assertions, which are well attested throughout Sanskrit literature going back to the Rigveda, the poet or bard impersonates the god and in that role praises, as it were, "himself," often with a quite blatant boastfulness that would seem like crude arrogance in a mere mortal. This kind of impersonation of a divinity is well known in literatures around the world, and in an earlier article I have tried to identify this widespread folk genre, to define its characteristics, and to give it a name.* It is in fact a prominent feature of the Bhagavad Gītā. When at 10.32 Kṛṣṇa says, "Arjuna, I am the beginning and the end of all created worlds, and I am their middle as well," this is not very different from the profoundly bold assertion attributed to Jesus at Revelation 1.8: "I am Alpha and Omega, the beginning and the ending, saith the Lord, which is, and which was, and which is to come, the almighty."

It is striking therefore that Kṛṣṇa's "self-praise," his *ātmastuti*, in Chapter 10 is immediately followed in the very next chapter by this astonishing vision of Kṛṣṇa as the monstrous (Sanskrit *ghora*) god of time. Here, in contrast with the elaborate sequence of "I am" assertions, Arjuna utters an equally elaborate sequence of "I see you" assertions (stanzas 11.15–31). Arjuna's song in praise of Kṛṣṇa arouses this most famous of responses from Kṛṣṇa, as we have already seen, at 11.32:

> I am time, the agent of the world's destruction, now grown old and set in motion to destroy the worlds. Even without you, all of these warriors arrayed in opposing battle-formation will cease to exist!

Kṛṣṇa then urges Arjuna to look around at the massive armies that he, Arjuna, and his brothers have assembled to fight the equally massive armies that his cousins have assembled against them. And Kṛṣṇa tells Arjuna with absolute, unsentimental certainty that he, Kṛṣṇa, has slain them already, long, long ago (stanza 11.33).

In fact Chapter 11 does not appear to fit well within its immediate context. Chapter 12 opens with Arjuna asking Kṛṣṇa to comment

*See George Thompson, "Ahaṃkāra and Ātmastuti: Self-assertion and Impersonation in the Rigveda," *History of Religions* 37, no. 2 (1997), pp. 141–71.

further on those who "have the best knowledge of yoga." As John Brockington has pointed out,* this passage seems to pick up immediately from Chapter 10. Brockington cites 10.10, where Kṛṣṇa offers to receive those who devote themselves to him with love and the yoga of insight. A few lines later (at 10.18), Arjuna asks for more insight into Kṛṣṇa's yoga and his divine powers. As we have seen, in the rest of Chapter 10 Kṛṣṇa reveals his divine powers to Arjuna, but he does not get around to a fuller explanation of yoga—that is, not until Chapter 12, where the discussion turns again to yoga as a means of attaining to Kṛṣṇa himself. It is as if Arjuna's vision of Kṛṣṇa as the terrible god of time in Chapter 11 had not occurred at all!

Ultimately, it may be impossible to decide with certainty whether Chapter 11 is an original part of the Bhagavad Gītā or a later insertion. The text contains so many apparent layers and internal contradictions that it is difficult to make a confident judgment about such matters. Nevertheless, the Bhagavad Gītā, no matter how it came to have the form that it now has, continues to be an enormously important document within the context of world literature. No one can any longer claim to be well-read and literate who has not read and responded thoughtfully to the very challenging questions that the Bhagavad Gītā asks of us about ourselves.

*See Brockington, *Sanskrit Epics*, p. 43, in Julius Lipner (ed.), *The Fruits of Our Desiring: An Enquiry into the Ethics of the Bhagavadgītā for Our Times* (Calgary: Bayeux Arts, 1997).

THE BHAGAVAD GITA

ONE

Dhṛtarāṣṭra spoke:

1. On the field of Dharma, on the field of the Kurus, they have assembled and are eager to fight, my men on one side and the sons of Pāṇḍu on the other. What did they do, Saṁjaya?

Saṁjaya spoke:

2. Your son Duryodhana saw the army of the Pāṇḍavas drawn up for battle, and then he, the king, approached his teacher, Droṇa, and spoke these words:
3. "My teacher, look at this magnificent army of Pāṇḍu's sons and their men all drawn up and led by your wise student, Dhṛṣṭadyumna, the son of Drupada!
4. There they are, warriors, great archers, all of them equal in battle to Bhīma and Arjuna, Yuyudhāna and Virāṭa, and Drupada as well, the great chariot warrior!
5. And Dhṛṣṭaketu and Cekitāna and the king of Kāśī, a heroic man! And also Purujit and Kuntibhoja, and that bull among men, the king of the Śibis!

6. Also there is that broad-striding Yudhamanyu, and Uttamaujas, also a hero, and Subhadra's son, and Draupadī's sons—all of them great chariot warriors!
7. And now notice, O best of the twice-born Brahmins, these others, the most distinguished among us, the leaders of my army: I tell you their names so that you will remember them![1]
8. You yourself, my lord Droṇa, and Bhīṣma and Karṇa, and Kṛpa, the winner of many battles! And Ashvatthama and Vikarṇa, and Somadatta's son as well!
9. And many other warriors willing to give up their lives for my sake, with their many weapons, all of them war-seasoned!
10. The strength of this army of ours is unmatched, led as it is by Bhīṣma, whereas that army of theirs, led as it is by Bhīma, can easily be matched![2]
11. And so in all of your strategic movements, stationed wherever you are ordered to be, may all of you, all of you, protect Bhīṣma!"
12. It delighted Duryodhana when the aged grandfather of the Kurus, Bhīṣma, roared out a lion's roar and blew his conch shell, full of fire.
13. Then conch shells and drums, and cymbals, and tabors and trumpets, all at once resounded. The sound was thunderous!
14. And standing there on their great chariot yoked to white stallions, Kṛṣṇa Mādhava and Arjuna, the son of Pāṇḍu, also blew their celestial conch shells.
15. Kṛṣṇa blew the horn that had belonged to Pañcajanya, Arjuna blew his Gift-of-God conch shell, and fierce wolf-bellied Bhīma blew the great Pauṇḍra horn.
16. Yudhiṣṭhira the king, the son of Kuntī, in turn blew the horn of endless victory, while Nakula and Sahadeva blew the sweet-toned and the jewel-toned conch shells.
17. The king of Kāśī, a master archer, and Śikandhin the great

chariot rider, and Dhṛṣṭadyumna, and Virāṭa and Sātyaki the unconquered,

18. and Drupada and the sons of Draupadī and the mighty-armed son of Subhadrā—all at once, my king, they all blew their conch shells, over and over again and in all directions!

19. That sound pierced the hearts of Dhṛtarāṣṭra's men, and the thunder of it made heaven and earth shake!

20. Then Arjuna, his war banner displaying the sign of the monkey, looked upon Dhṛtarāṣṭra's men, just as the clashing of the weapons was to begin. And then the son of Pāṇḍu raised his bow.

21. And, my king, he spoke these words to Kṛṣṇa: "O unshakable one, stop my chariot here in the middle, between these two armies,

22. where I can see these men fixed in their positions and eager to fight, these men who are ready to fight against me in the strain of war.

23. I see them gathered here, these men who are set to fight, hungry to please in battle Dhṛtarāṣṭra's reckless son."

24. O Bhārata, Kṛṣṇa heard the words that Arjuna spoke, and he stopped that excellent chariot between the two armies.

25. Standing before Bhīṣma and Droṇa and all of the great kings, Kṛṣṇa spoke: "Arjuna, here they are, the assembled Kurus. Look at them!"

26. Arjuna looked upon them there where they stood, fathers and grandfathers, teachers, uncles and brothers, sons and grandsons, and companions,

27. fathers-in-law and dear friends, in both of the armies. Seeing them all standing there, his kinsmen,

28. Arjuna was overwhelmed by deep compassion, and in despair he said, "Kṛṣṇa, yes, I see my kinsmen gathered here and ready to fight.

29. My arms and legs have grown heavy. My mouth is dry. My body is trembling, and the hair on my head stands on end.

30. My Gāṇḍīva bow drops from my hand, and my skin—it burns. I cannot stand still, and my mind swirls like a storm.
31. Kṛṣṇa, I see unfavorable signs here, and I can see nothing good in killing my own family in battle!
32. I have no desire for victory, Kṛṣṇa, nor for a kingdom, nor for the joys of life. What is a kingdom to us, Kṛṣṇa, and what are pleasures, or life itself?
33. It is for our kinsmen that we have desired a kingdom, pleasures, and the joys of life, these men assembled here in battle, men who are prepared to give up their lives and their fortunes.
34. Our teachers, our fathers and sons, and our grandfathers as well. Uncles, fathers-in-law, grandsons, brothers-in-law, all of them our kinsmen!
35. I do not want to kill them, even if they kill me, Kṛṣṇa, not for kingship over all of the three worlds, much less for the earth itself!
36. What joy would there be for us, Kṛṣṇa, if we kill Dhṛtarāṣṭra and his men? Evil will follow us if we kill them, even as they draw their bows against us.
37. Thus it is not right for us to kill Dhṛtarāṣṭra's men. They are our own kin! How can we win happiness, Kṛṣṇa, if we kill our own kin?
38. Even if they themselves don't see it, blinded as they are by the greed that has destroyed their reason, it is wrong to destroy one's family and to betray one's friends.
39. How could we not have the wisdom to turn away from this evil thing, since we can see that to destroy the whole family is a terrible crime?
40. If our family is destroyed, then the timeless traditional laws of the family will die too. If traditional law dies, then chaos will overwhelm the entire family.[3]
41. If the family is overwhelmed by chaos, then the women of the family will be corrupted, and when the women are corrupted, Kṛṣṇa, all social order will collapse.

42. This collapse drags the family and those who destroy it down into hell, and their ancestors fall with them, since the offerings of rice and water will no longer be given.
43. The crimes of those who destroy the family cause the social order to collapse. They undermine the unchanging laws of caste duty and family duty.
44. Kṛṣṇa, we have been taught that a place in hell is saved for men who undermine family duty. This is our tradition.
45. No! We are intent on committing a great evil here, driven as we are, by greed for a kingdom and for pleasures, to kill our own kinsmen!
46. If Dhṛtarāṣṭra's men with all their weapons were to kill me here as I am, unarmed and unresisting, that would bring me greater peace."
47. Saying these things in the midst of a war, Arjuna sank down into his chariot seat. He dropped his bow and arrows. His mind was tormented by grief.

TWO

Saṁjaya spoke:

1. Arjuna sat there overwhelmed by compassion, his eyes blurred and filled with tears. And then Kṛṣṇa spoke these words to him:

The Blessed One spoke:

2. Where does this weakness in you come from, Arjuna, at this time of crisis? It is not fitting in a nobleman. It does not gain you heaven. It does not bring you any honor.
3. Don't give in to this impotence! It doesn't belong in you. Give up this petty weakness, this faintness of heart. You are a world conqueror, Arjuna. Stand up!

Arjuna spoke:

4. But how can I engage Bhīṣma and Droṇa in battle, Kṛṣṇa? How can I fight them with my arrows, these two men who both deserve my devotion instead?
5. No, instead of killing my gurus, these men of great authority, it would be better for me to eat the food of a beggar here in this world. If I were to kill my gurus here, even though they seek

their own ends against me, it would be like eating food smeared with blood.

6. And we do not know which is the heavier burden: whether we should win the fight, or whether they should win. Dhṛtarāṣṭra's men stand there, drawn up before us. If we were to kill them, we ourselves would no longer wish to live!
7. This grief that I feel seems like a sickness that strikes at my very being. I ask you, because my understanding of duty is confused. What would be better? Explain this to me clearly. I am your student. Your are my refuge. Teach me!
8. Even if I could attain unrivaled wealth on this earth and a prosperous kingdom and lordship over the gods, I still would not be able to see what might dispel this sorrow that burns my senses.

Saṁjaya spoke:

9. So Arjuna, the conqueror, spoke. "I will not fight!" he said to Kṛṣṇa, and having spoken thus, he became silent.
10. O lord of the Bhāratas, Kṛṣṇa then responded, it seemed with a smile, as Arjuna sat there despondently between the two armies. These were his words.

The Blessed One spoke:

11. You grieve for those who are beyond grieving, and you talk like one with wisdom, but the truly learned grieve neither for those who have lost their lives nor for those who still have them.
12. But in fact there never was a time when I did not exist, nor you, nor any of these other lords. And there never will be a time when we do not exist.
13. Just as the embodied one[1] experiences childhood, and youth, and old age, in this body, in the same way he enters other bodies. A wise man is not disturbed by this.

14. O Arjuna, encounters with the material world induce sensations of cold and heat and pleasure and pain. They come and they go. They are impermanent. You are a Bhārata! Endure them!
15. Arjuna, these sensations do not make a wise man waver, for whom pain and pleasure are the same. Such a man is fit for immortality!
16. What does not exist cannot come into existence, and what does exist cannot cease to exist, but that place where existence and nonexistence meet can be seen by those who see things as they are.
17. But know that this is imperishable, this which pervades the whole world. No one can destroy what is imperishable!
18. It is said that our bodies come to an end. But they belong to an embodied one[2] who is unending, who does not perish, and who is beyond all measure. For this reason, Arjuna, you should fight!
19. Whoever thinks that this one here is a killer, or who thinks that he has been killed, in both cases he is wrong. For indeed he does not kill, nor is he himself ever killed.[3]
20. He is not born, nor does he die—in any way! Once one exists, one can never not exist! Unborn, eternal, permanent, primordial—one is not killed when the body is killed!
21. One who knows that this is imperishable and eternal, unborn and unchanging, Arjuna, how can such a person kill, or cause anyone else to kill?
22. Just as a man discards worn-out clothes and gets others that are new, so the embodied one[4] discards worn-out bodies and enters others that are new.
23. Weapons do not cut him, fire does not burn him, the waters do not wet him, the wind does not dry him out.
24. He cannot be cut or burned, he cannot be made wet or dried out: he is unchanging, all-pervading, immovable, and eternal.
25. He is called the unmanifest, the inconceivable, the immutable.

Therefore, once you have understood that this is so, you should not mourn for him.

26. But even if you think that he is constantly born and constantly dies, even then, Arjuna, you should not mourn for him.
27. For death is certain for anyone who has been born, just as birth is certain for anyone who has died. Since this condition cannot be avoided, you should not mourn.
28. The origins of all things are inaccessible to us. Here in the midst of life, Arjuna, things are accessible. But the ends of all things are also inaccessible to us. So what is there to lament?
29. It is a rare and wonderful thing when someone sees him,[5] rare and wonderful when one speaks of him, rare and wonderful also when one hears of him. But in fact to have heard is not the same as to have known him.
30. The embodied one,[6] who dwells in the body of each of us, is completely beyond harm. Therefore, Arjuna, you should not mourn for any being whatsoever.
31. Also, you should reflect upon your own caste duties.[7] You should not get agitated. In fact, for a warrior there is nothing more noble than a just war.
32. The opportunity arises by pure chance, and the doors of heaven open. O Arjuna, those warriors are happy who get the opportunity to fight such a war!
33. But if you will not participate in this just war, a war of duty,[8] you will have abandoned your caste duty and your honor as well, and you will have won only evil for yourself.
34. The whole world will talk of your permanent dishonor, and for someone of your stature dishonor is worse than death.
35. These great chariot warriors will think that you have fled from the battle out of fear, and you will become a small, despised man among men who once thought highly of you!

36. Your enemies will say many scandalous things and they will ridicule your competence in war. What could be more disgraceful?
37. If you are killed, you will win heaven. If you are victorious, you will have the world to enjoy. Therefore, stand up, Arjuna! Don't hesitate! Fight!
38. Joy and suffering, success and failure, victory and defeat: treat them all alike. Brace yourself for battle. In this way you will avoid dishonor!
39. This insight[9] has been presented to you in the form of Sāṁkhya philosophy. Now hear it in the form of yoga tradition. Disciplined by this insight, Arjuna, you will escape from the bonds of action.
40. Progress in yoga is never wasted, and it is never unproductive. Even a little effort in the practice of yoga[10] saves you from the great terror of life.
41. This insight[11] based on firm resolve is unique and whole. Arjuna, men who have no resolve have poor insight. They veer endlessly in all directions.
42. Some people please themselves by debating the Vedas. They recite the florid Vedic chants, but they have no insight, while ever saying that only the Vedas matter!
43. In their hearts they are driven by desire and are eager for heaven. Their words promise rebirth as the fruit of their actions. Their talk is all about their elaborate rituals whose purpose is to gain pleasure and power.
44. They are obsessed with pleasure and power! The words of the Vedas deprive them of good sense. They lack the insight that is based on firm resolve, and they do not gain insight even when engaged in intense concentration.[12]
45. The world of the Vedas is the natural world with its three conditions. Arjuna, live in the world that is beyond this one, free of

its conditions and dualities. Remain always within this true world, free from both the exertion for wealth and the enjoyment of it. Remain within the self.[13]

46. As useful as a water tank is when there is flooding in all directions, that is how useful all of the Vedas[14] are for a Brahmin[15] who has true insight.
47. Focus your mind on action alone, but never on the fruits of your actions. Your goal should never be the fruits of your actions, nor should you be attached to nonaction.
48. Practice yoga and perform the actions that you are obliged to do, but, Arjuna, don't be attached to them. Treat success and failure alike. This kind of even-mindedness is called yoga.
49. Arjuna, action is far inferior to the yoga of insight. Seek refuge in insight. Those whose goal is the fruits of their actions wind up miserable.
50. A man who is committed to insight leaves behind both good actions and bad. Therefore, commit yourself to yoga, for yoga is skillfulness in all action.
51. Those who are committed to insight, who are wise, renounce the fruit that is born of action. Freed from the bonds of rebirth, they go to a place where there is no misery.
52. When your insight transcends this jungle of delusion, then you will become indifferent to what you have been taught by Vedic tradition and whatever you will be taught.
53. When your insight, which has been distracted by the traditional teachings, finally stands unwavering, motionless in concentration, then you will reach yoga.

Arjuna spoke:

54. Kṛṣṇa, how do you describe someone who is stable in this wisdom, who can stay fixed in concentration? How would such a person speak, how would he sit, how would he go about in this world?

The Blessed One spoke:

55. Arjuna, when one gives up all the desires that fill the mind, when one is content with oneself in one's *ātman*, then one is said to be stable in this wisdom.
56. When bad fortune no longer disturbs his mind, and when good fortune no longer excites him, then you could call this person a sage, stable in this wisdom, in whom longing and fear and anger have vanished.
57. When he feels no desire whatsoever, and no matter what good or bad happens to him, he does not delight in or hate it, such a person has wisdom that is stable.
58. When he withdraws his senses from all sensuous things, like a tortoise that draws it legs into its shell, then his wisdom is stable.
59. The fascination of sense objects withdraws from the embodied one who gives up food. For him, only the flavor, the trace of the flavor, lingers. And once he has seen the highest, that leaves him too.
60. Arjuna, even an intelligent man who strives to control his senses can be tormented by them. They can attack him and violently seize his mind.
61. He should restrain all of his senses and, committed to yoga, he should sit, intent on me. If his senses are under control, then his wisdom will be stable.
62. When a man meditates on sensual objects, attachment to them develops in him, and this attachment produces desire, and this desire produces anger.
63. From this anger comes delusion, and from this delusion comes the distortion of memory, and this distortion of memory leads to the loss of insight. From this, one dies.
64. But when a man approaches sensual objects with his own senses detached from desire and anger, that is, when his senses are

controlled by his *ātman*, then he is in control of himself[16] and he finds peace.

65. In that peace, all of his sorrows vanish, for as soon as his thoughts become tranquil, his insight becomes steady.
66. An undisciplined man has no insight. An undisciplined man has no effective power, and without this power he has no peace. And without peace how can he be happy?
67. For the senses wander, and when one lets the mind follow them, it carries wisdom away like a windblown ship on the waters.
68. Therefore, great warrior, the one who has withdrawn his senses entirely from the things of the senses has steadfast wisdom.
69. When it is nighttime for all creatures, the one who is self-restrained is awake. And when all others are awake, it is night-time for that sage who sees truly.[17]
70. Just as the waters that enter the ocean do not fill it nor do they disturb its depths, so too is the peace of the one into whom all these desires pour. The man who is driven by desire does not know such peace.
71. The man who abandons all desires, who goes about free from cravings, for whom there is no talk of "mine!" or "me!"—he finds peace.
72. This, Arjuna, is the divine state of Brahman. Having attained this, one is no longer confused. When one abides in this state, even at the moment of death, one attains the sublime peace of Brahman.[18]

THREE

Arjuna spoke:

1. Kṛṣṇa, if you think that insight is more powerful than action, then why do you urge me to engage in such a terrible action as this?
2. With words that seem convoluted you have confused my mind! Please tell me the one thing I need to know to attain the highest good.

The Blessed One spoke:

3. O blameless one, long ago I taught that there are two paths to the highest good. For the followers of Sāṁkhya, it is attained by means of the yoga of knowledge. For yogins it is attained by means of the yoga of action.[1]
4. A man does not go beyond action by merely avoiding action, nor does he achieve spiritual success by renunciation alone.
5. For no one exists even for a moment without performing actions. Even if unwillingly, every one of us must act, due to the forces of nature.
6. A man can control the senses by which he acts, but if he sits

while still recalling in his mind all of the attractions of the senses, then he fools himself. He is known as a hypocrite.

7. But whoever controls his senses with his mind, and with all of his ability engages in the yoga of action, such a person is unattached, Arjuna. He is distinguished among men.
8. You should perform the actions that you are obliged to perform, because action is better than inaction. Without action, you would not be able to maintain your body's health. It would surely fail.
9. This world is in bondage to action except when it is performed as a sacrifice. You should remain unattached, Arjuna, and continue to perform action that is intended as sacrifice.
10. Long ago Prajāpati, the Lord of Creation,[2] brought forth all creatures along with sacrifice, and he said, "By means of sacrifice you will grow and multiply. Let sacrifice be your wish-fulfilling cow!
11. Make the gods flourish by means of it, and let the gods make you flourish as well! Make yourselves flourish for each other's sake. You will reach the highest good.
12. For the gods will give you the things that you desire, because your sacrifices have made them flourish. Whoever enjoys their gifts without giving in return is little more than a thief."
13. Good men who eat the remnants of such sacrifice are released from all guilt. But those who cook only for themselves without offering sacrifice are evil men who eat what is evil.
14. All creatures grow because of food. Food grows because of Parjanya.[3] Parjanya grows because of sacrifice. And sacrifice grows because of action.
15. Know that action arises from Brahman and that Brahman arises from the imperishable syllable OM. Therefore, the Brahman that pervades the universe is established permanently in sacrifice.[4]
16. So the wheel is set in motion, and whoever does not keep it turning, Arjuna, is sinful and addicted to sensual pleasures. He lives a meaningless life.

17. But the man who takes pleasure only in the self,[5] and is satisfied only with the self, and finds his contentment in the self alone—for him there is nothing at all to do!
18. For him there is no purpose whatsoever in what he has done or in what he hasn't done. Nor does he depend on other creatures at all to give purpose to his life.
19. Therefore, continue to do any action that you are obliged to do, but always without attachment. By continuing to act without attachment, a man attains the highest good.
20. Janaka and the other ancient kings attained complete success by means of action alone. You too should act, Arjuna, while pursuing only the protection of the world.
21. Whatever the best among us does, the rest will also do. The world always follows the standard that the best among us sets.
22. Arjuna, there is nothing whatsoever that I need to do in any of the three worlds, heaven, air, and earth. There is nothing to gain that I have not already gained, and yet I am still engaged in action.
23. If I myself did not engage in action relentlessly at every moment, Arjuna, all mankind would surely follow in my path.
24. All these worlds would collapse if I myself did not perform my work.[6] I would thus become an agent of caste confusion, and I would wind up destroying all of these creatures.
25. Just as the ignorant who are attached to their actions continue to act, so the man of knowledge also acts, though without attachment, since he pursues the protection of the world.
26. The man of knowledge should not confuse the understanding of the ignorant who are attached to action. Like one disciplined in yoga, he should let them take pleasure in their actions.
27. Actions are performed at all times as a result of the three conditions of nature.[7] The man whose self is deluded because of his egotism thinks, "I am the actor."
28. But when he truly understands the difference between action and

the conditions of nature, then, Arjuna, he thinks, "These conditions arise from other conditions." He is not attached to them.

29. People who are confused about the conditions of nature are attached to them and to the actions that follow from them. One who knows the whole truth should not upset the slow-witted[8] ones who know only a part.
30. Surrender all your actions to me, and fix your mind on your inmost self. Become free from desire and possessiveness. Cast off this fever and fight!
31. Men who always follow this teaching of mine, confident in it and not disputing it, are freed from their actions.
32. But know that those who dispute my teaching and do not follow it—they misunderstand all knowledge, they are senseless, they are lost!
33. One behaves according to one's own nature—even the one who knows his nature! All creatures follow their own nature. No one can stop that!
34. Attraction and aversion await every single object of the senses. One should not come under their control, for they are bandits lying in waiting.
35. One's own duty[9] done poorly is better than another's duty done well. It is better to die engaged in one's own duty. Taking on another's duty is dangerous.

Arjuna spoke:

36. Then what makes a man commit evil against his own will, Kṛṣṇa, as if driven to it by force?

The Blessed One spoke:

37. It is desire, it is anger, and it arises from the condition of passion.[10] It is an all-consuming mouth and a great evil. Know that this is the enemy!

38. As the fire is obscured by smoke and the mirror by stains, as the embryo is enveloped by the membrane, so this world is obscured by that desire.
39. And knowledge is obscured by it as well, Arjuna! That perpetual enemy of the wise man takes the form of desire and is an insatiable fire.
40. The senses, the mind, insight—these are its foundation. By means of them desire confuses the embodied self and obscures knowledge.
41. Therefore, Arjuna, you must control the senses first, and then strike down that evil that destroys knowledge and discrimination.
42. They say that the senses are superior to sense objects, but truly the mind is superior to the senses. And indeed insight is superior to the mind. But there is the one who is superior even to insight.
43. Gain insight into this one who is beyond insight, and find the stability of the self by means of the self. O Arjuna, strike the enemy who takes the form of desire and is formidable.

FOUR

The Blessed One spoke:

1. I taught this eternal yoga tradition to Vivasvat, the god of the sun. Vivasvat taught it to Manu, the Father of mankind. Manu himself taught it to Ikṣvāku, the first king.
2. The royal seers knew this tradition, which was handed down from one to the other, but after a long passage of time, Arjuna, it became lost.
3. This ancient yoga tradition is what I teach to you today, for you are my devotee and my friend, and this is the deepest of mysteries.

Arjuna spoke:

4. Vivasvat's birth occurred a long time ago. You were born much later. How should I understand what you mean when you say that you taught this teaching in the beginning?

The Blessed One spoke:

5. I have passed through many births, and so have you, Arjuna. But I can recall them all, whereas you, Arjuna, cannot.

6. I am unborn, and my self is eternal, and I am the lord of all beings. Nevertheless, I take part in nature and I manifest myself by means of my own power.[1]
7. Whenever religious duty wanes, Arjuna, and its opposite, chaos,[2] waxes strong, then I release myself into the world.
8. In age after age, I manifest myself in order to protect the virtuous, to destroy those who do harm, and to reestablish religious duty.
9. The one who truly knows that my birth and my action are divine does not return for another birth, when he abandons the body at death. Arjuna, he returns to me!
10. Many people have been purified by the fire of knowledge. They no longer feel passion or fear or anger. They belong to me and take their refuge in me. In the end they all come to me.
11. Those who come to me, no matter how they do so—I grant them my grace. Arjuna, all men universally[3] follow my path.
12. They hope for success in their actions, so they sacrifice here to the gods, because here in the world of mankind success comes quickly from acts of sacrifice.
13. I created the four castes of the world, distinguishing them according to their qualities and their actions. And though I am the agent of this world, know that I am also the eternal nonagent.
14. Actions do not defile me. You will not find any desire in me for the fruits of action. One who understands this about me is not imprisoned by his own actions.
15. Knowing this, the ancient ones performed the actions that they were obliged to do, even as they strove eagerly toward liberation. Therefore, you too should perform all obligatory actions, just like the ancient ones before you!
16. What is action? What is nonaction? Even the sages were confused about this. I will now explain to you what action is, since knowing this will free you from your misery.

17. You should understand what action is and distinguish it from wrong action. And from these you must distinguish nonaction. The path of action is hard to understand!
18. He who is able to see the nonaction within action, and the action within nonaction, is truly full of wisdom among men. He performs all obligatory actions, but he is disciplined in yoga.
19. A man whose endeavors are free from the manipulations of desire sacrifices his actions in the fire of knowledge. The wise call him a learned man.
20. Giving up his attachment to the fruits of his actions, always content, dependent on nothing—even when he engages in action, he himself does not really act at all.
21. When he has abandoned hope, and has restrained himself and his thoughts, when he has abandoned all of his possessions, then it is only his body that acts;[4] he does not accumulate guilt.
22. Content with whatever chance brings to him, he has passed beyond duality. He knows no envy. He is even-tempered whether in success or in failure. Even when he does act, he is not imprisoned by his actions!
23. When a man is unattached and free of all of this, when his thoughts are rooted firmly in knowledge, when he performs his actions in the spirit of sacrifice, his actions are completely dissolved!
24. The offering is this infinite Brahman. The oblation is this infinite Brahman. It is Brahman that pours the oblation into the fire of Brahman. One attains to Brahman by concentrating completely on the action of Brahman![5]
25. Some yogins engage only in sacrifices to the gods. Others sacrifice symbolically by pouring their oblations into the fire of infinite Brahman.[6]

26. Some yogins pour the senses into the fire of self-restraint, withdrawing their hearing and their other senses. Yet others pour sound and the other sense objects into the fire of the senses.
27. And others offer all of the actions of the senses, the actions of the breath and the other actions, into the fire of the yoga of self-control which is ignited by knowledge.
28. Some sacrifice material objects, others practice austerities, and still others practice yoga. Some sacrifice through their knowledge and their study of the Vedas. These are all devout men committed to keeping their sacred vows.
29. Others engage in the practice of breath control[7] by checking the course of the inhaled breath and the exhaled breath. Thus they pour the inhaled breath into the exhaled, and the exhaled breath into the inhaled.
30. Others refrain from eating, instead pouring their breaths into the cosmic breaths.[8] All of these people know the meaning of sacrifice. Sacrifice destroys impurities.
31. There are men who eat the remnants of the sacrifice, the nectar of immortality. They go to the eternal Brahman. This world does not belong to the man who does not sacrifice, Arjuna! How then could the next world be his?
32. In this way the many forms of sacrifice are spread out as an offering before Brahman. Know that they are all born from action. Knowing this you will be free!
33. But, Arjuna, the sacrifice of knowledge[9] is higher than the sacrifice of material things. All action without exception culminates in knowledge.
34. Learn this, Arjuna, by submitting humbly to one's teachers, by asking them thoughtful questions, by serving them. They are men of knowledge and they have seen the truth. They will pass their knowledge on to you.

35. When you have learned this, Arjuna, you will never encounter delusion again. By means of this knowledge you will come to see fully that all beings are in yourself and thus in me.
36. Even if you were the most sinful among all sinners, with the help of this ship of knowledge you will cross over all of this sorrow.
37. Just as fire, once it is kindled, reduces the firewood to ashes, in the very same way, Arjuna, the fire of knowledge reduces all of your actions to ashes!
38. You will not find anywhere in this world a means of purification that is the equal of knowledge. A man who has been perfected by yoga in time will find knowledge within himself.
39. A man of faith, intent only upon this knowledge, his senses well restrained, will obtain it, and once he has obtained it, he soon reaches supreme peace.
40. But a man who does not have this knowledge and faith will perish, his soul filled with doubts. And filled with doubts as he is, there will be no joy for him either in this world or the next.
41. Arjuna, actions do not bind the man who renounces his actions through yoga, who severs doubt by means of knowledge, who is in full possession of himself.
42. Therefore, with this sword of knowledge, sever this doubt that rests in your heart, Arjuna, this doubt of yours that arises from ignorance. Stand up, then, and stand upon yoga!

FIVE

Arjuna spoke:

1. You praise the renunciation[1] of actions, Kṛṣṇa, and then again you praise yoga as a means of action. Please tell me with all certainty which of these is the better course?

The Blessed One spoke:

2. Renunciation of action and the yoga of action both lead to the highest good, but of the two the yoga of action is better than the renunciation of action.
3. One who does not hate and who does not desire is understood to be a permanent *saṁnyāsin.* Because he is beyond dualisms, Arjuna, he is easily freed from his bondage.
4. It is only the foolish who declare that Sāṁkhya philosophy and yoga discipline are different schools. The learned do not say this. A man who is focused completely on either one will find the fruit of both.
5. Practitioners of yoga arrive at the same position that practitioners of Sāṁkhya philosophy reach. Whoever can see that Sāṁkhya and yoga are a single discipline sees truly.

6. But, Arjuna, renunciation is difficult to attain without yogic discipline, whereas a sage who is disciplined in yoga quickly reaches infinite Brahman.
7. Once he becomes disciplined in yoga, the self[2] becomes purified, the self becomes controlled, and his senses become subdued. The self becomes united with the self of all creatures. Whatever he does in this state does not stain him.
8. "I who am not doing anything," he should think to himself, the man who is disciplined in yoga, and who knows the true nature of things. Meanwhile, he sees, he hears, he touches, he smells, he eats, he goes, he sleeps, he breathes,
9. he talks, he relieves himself, he takes with his hands, he opens his eyes, he closes his eyes—but always he holds firm to the thought, "This is merely the senses interacting with sense objects."
10. He gives his actions over to infinite Brahman and abandons attachment. When he acts in this way, guilt does not adhere to him, just as water does not adhere to the lotus leaf.
11. Yogins perform actions with body and mind and insight, and with the senses as well, but since they have abandoned attachment, they perform these actions only for the purification of the self.
12. The undisciplined man is attached to the fruits of his action and is in bondage to the desire that causes them. But the disciplined man abandons the fruits of his actions and thereby attains abiding peace.
13. In his mind he renounces all actions. The embodied one sits easily, in control, within that city of the nine gates that is his body, neither acting nor causing others to act.
14. The lord does not engender the world's agency or actions or the perpetual union of the world's actions with their fruits. These arise autonomously, out of their own nature.
15. The ever-present lord does not take on the effects of anyone's

misfortune nor anyone's good fortune. Knowledge of him is obscured by ignorance. All peoples are deluded by it.

16. But whenever this ignorance among men is destroyed by knowledge of the self, then like the sun their knowledge illuminates that supreme realm of Brahman.
17. That is their insight, that is their true self. That is their foundation and their ultimate goal. They reach that state of no return where their sins are dispelled by knowledge.
18. Learned men look upon an educated and cultured Brahmin just as they look upon a cow or an elephant or a dog, or even a low-caste dog-eater.
19. This created world is conquered by those who maintain the mind in equanimity. And indeed for them the world of Brahman is a flawless equilibrium, and as a result they dwell in Brahman.
20. One should not take pleasure in getting what one wants, nor should one reject getting what one does not want. One's insight is steady. One is not confused. One knows Brahman and dwells in it.
21. When one is no longer attached to contact with external objects, one finds pleasure within oneself. The self is disciplined by *brahmayoga*,[3] and one reaches a pleasure that is imperishable.
22. For the delights that arise from external objects are really wombs of misery. They all have a beginning and an end, Arjuna. A wise man takes no pleasure in them.
23. The man who is able to overcome the agitation that comes with desire and anger, here in this world, before he leaves the body—he is a disciplined man, he is a happy man.
24. Such a man contains his pleasure and his joy within himself. His light is within himself and nowhere else. Such a man is a yogin who has become one with Brahman. He has reached the sublime peace of Brahman.

25. Seers who destroy their sins, who cut through all doubt, who are masters of themselves, attain this sublime peace of Brahman, delighting in the welfare of all beings.
26. The sublime peace of Brahman is always present for those devoted men who have freed themselves from desire and anger, who have tamed their minds and have come to know themselves.
27. The sage shuns external objects and fixes his gaze between the eyebrows. He balances the inhaled breath with the exhaled breath as they pass through the nostrils.
28. His senses, his thoughts, and his insights are all restrained. This sage is committed to his liberation. In him, desire and fear and anger have vanished. He is what he always has been. He is free.
29. Know that it is I who am the enjoyer of sacrifices and austerities. It is I who am the great lord of all worlds and the heart's friend of all beings. Know this and find peace.

SIX

The Blessed One spoke:

1. Whoever does not concern himself with the fruits of action and yet performs the actions that he is obliged to do is both a *saṁnyāsin* and a yogin. Whoever neglects his ritual fires and his ritual obligations is not.[1]
2. Arjuna, know that what people call renunciation is really yoga, for no one becomes a yogin who has not renounced personal intention.
3. For a sage who seeks to advance in yoga, action is said to be the instrument, whereas for a sage who has already advanced in yoga, serenity is said to be the instrument.
4. One is said to be advanced in yoga when one has renounced all personal intention and when one is no longer attached to sense objects and actions.
5. One should lift oneself up by means of the self. Do not degrade the self, for the self is one's only friend, and at the same time the self is one's only foe.
6. The self is one's friend when one has conquered the self by

means of the self. But when a man neglects the self, then, like an enemy at war, that very self will turn against him.

7. A peaceful man who has mastered himself has a higher self that is deeply concentrated, whether in cold or in heat, whether in pleasure or in pain, whether in honor or in disgrace.
8. Such a man has a self that delights in knowledge and discrimination. He stands on the mountaintop. He has conquered his senses. He is called a yogin because he is disciplined. A clod of earth, a rock, a piece of gold—for such a man, it's all the same.
9. He is distinguished among men because he regards them all as the same: a friend, an ally, a foreigner, a bystander, a neutral party, an enemy, a kinsman—whether good men or evil!
10. A yogin should always discipline himself. He should dwell in a remote place, alone, restraining his thoughts and himself, without hopes and without ambitions.
11. He should prepare for himself a firm seat[2] in a purified place that is neither too high nor too low, a seat that is covered by a sacred cloth, a deerskin, and *kuśa* grass.
12. There he should fix his mind on a single object and restrain the activity of his thoughts and senses. Sitting in that seat he should practice yoga for the purification of the self.
13. He should be steadfast, holding his body, his head, and his neck straight and motionless. He should focus his gaze on the tip of his nose and keep his gaze from wandering.
14. With the self at peace and all fears gone, he should hold firm to his vow of celibacy. He should sit, in full control of his mind, with his thoughts on me, disciplined, intent on me.
15. A yogin who disciplines himself vigilantly in this way, controlling his mind, attains the peace that culminates in *nirvāṇa*,[3] the peace that rests in me.
16. Yoga is not the path for someone who eats too much, nor for

someone who refuses to eat at all.[4] Nor, Arjuna, is it the path for someone who sleeps too much, or someone who stays too much awake.

17. The yoga that destroys sorrow is the path for someone disciplined in his eating and his playing, disciplined in his performance of the actions that he is obliged to do, disciplined both in the dream state and in wakefulness.
18. One is said to be disciplined in yoga when one's craving for all of the pleasures of the world is gone, and when one's thoughts are controlled and focused only on the self.
19. Like a lamp where there is no wind, he does not waver. This is the traditional image of the yogin whose mind is restrained and who practices the yoga of the self.
20. When his thinking settles down and comes to rest, checked by the practice of yoga, and when he sees the self by means of the self alone, he takes pleasure only in the self.
21. The endless joy that is beyond the senses and can be perceived only with insight—when he knows this steadfastly, he never wanders from this truth.
22. And when he has obtained this truth, he understands that there is nothing greater to be obtained than this. When he is steadfast in this truth, no sorrow disturbs him, no matter how heavy it is to endure.
23. He should know that this is what yoga is: to undo the bonds that bind us to sorrow. It should be practiced with determination and without the despair that troubles one's thoughts.
24. He should abandon all desires, without exception, that arise from self-interest. He should completely restrain the crowd of the senses with his mind.
25. Slowly but surely he should settle down and come to rest, with insight that is held firmly. He should direct his mind to the self. He should reflect upon nothing whatsoever.

26. Wherever the unstable wavering mind wanders off to, he should withdraw his mind from there, and bring it under control within himself.
27. For supreme joy comes to the yogin whose mind is at peace. This yogin has pacified his passion, he has merged with Brahman, he is without stain.
28. In this way, constantly disciplining himself, the yogin has freed himself from stain. He easily attains the endless joy that comes from contact with Brahman.
29. Having yoked himself by means of yoga, he sees the self that dwells in all beings and all beings within the self. Indeed, he sees the same in all things.
30. Whoever sees me everywhere and sees everything in me will never be separated from me, nor will I be separated from him.
31. The yogin who is aware of the oneness of life is devoted to me, the one who dwells in all beings. Wherever he happens to find himself, he remains within me.
32. Arjuna, whoever sees the identity in all beings by comparing them all to the self within him—whether there is joy or sorrow there—I think of such a man as a highest yogin.

Arjuna spoke:

33. You have explained yoga to me as equanimity in all things. But, Kṛṣṇa, I cannot see how this can be firmly established, because of all this restlessness.
34. The mind is restless, Kṛṣṇa. It is violent, strong, and stubborn. I think that restraining it is very difficult, like restraining the wind!

The Blessed One spoke:

35. No doubt, Arjuna! The mind is difficult to control, and restless. But, Arjuna, with rigorous practice and dispassion one can restrain it.

36. Yoga is difficult to practice for one who cannot control himself. That is my view as well. But a man who can control himself, and who strives, is capable of practicing yoga, by using the right means.

Arjuna spoke:

37. Someone who has faith but does not strive, and whose mind frequently wanders away from yogic practice, will not achieve success in yoga. Kṛṣṇa, what path does he take?
38. Hasn't he fallen away from both yoga and self-control, and doesn't he perish like a cloud cut in two? Kṛṣṇa, he has no foundation, and on the path that leads to Brahman, he is utterly deluded.
39. Kṛṣṇa, please, you can cut through this doubt of mine completely. There is no one but you who can cut through this doubt!

The Blessed One spoke:

40. Arjuna, my friend, neither in this world nor in the next does that one perish, for anyone who has done some measure of good cannot possibly take the wrong path!
41. He goes to the worlds that he has made with his good actions, and he dwells in them for endless years. Then the man who has strayed away from yoga is reborn into a house of the pure and the blessed.
42. Or else he is born instead into a family of enlightened yogins, for such a birth is even harder to obtain in this world.
43. There he obtains the kind of understanding that he had gained from his previous body. And then, Arjuna, joy of the Kurus, he strives further toward perfection.
44. For he is carried along, beyond his own control, by the power of his previous practice. Anyone who merely desires to know yoga transcends Vedic recitations about Brahman.

45. When he strives with great effort, the yogin becomes purified of his faults, and over the course of many births he becomes perfected. Then finally he takes the highest path.
46. The yogin is considered superior to ascetics who practice austerity, superior to men of knowledge, and superior also to men of action. Therefore, Arjuna, become a yogin!
47. But among all yogins, the one who places his faith in me, who devotes[5] himself to me, who has gone to me with his inmost self—I judge him to be the most disciplined of all!

SEVEN

The Blessed One spoke:

1. Focus your mind on me, Arjuna, rely on me, and commit yourself to yoga. Hear how you will come to know me, completely, without any doubt.
2. I will tell you what knowledge is, and what discrimination is. And once you have known these, there will be nothing more to know.
3. Among thousands of men only one may strive for success, and among those who strive thus and succeed, perhaps only one will truly know me.
4. My physical nature consists of eight parts: earth, water, fire, and air; and then space and mind, intelligence, and ego-sense.
5. But this is my lower nature. You should know that I have a higher nature as well, Arjuna. It is the life-force that sustains this world.
6. It is the womb of all beings. Consider this well, Arjuna. I am the origin of this entire world, and I am its dissolution as well.
7. There is nothing whatsoever beyond me, Arjuna! All this world is strung on me like rows of pearls on a string.

8. I am the taste, the essence, in the waters, Arjuna. I am the light in the sun and the moon. I am the sacred OM in all of the Vedas. I am the sound in space. I am the manhood in men.
9. I am the sweet scent of the earth as well, and I am the radiance in fire, the life in all beings, and I am the ascetic heat in holy men.
10. Know, Arjuna, that I am the eternal seed in all beings. I am the insight of the insightful. I am the brilliance of brilliant men.
11. I am also the strength of strong men, the strength that is free from desire and passion. And I am that desire in all beings, Arjuna, that does not resist duty!
12. There are states of clarity, states of passion, and states of inertia. Know that they come only from me. But I am not in them. They are in me![1]
13. These states consist of the three conditions of nature. The entire world is deluded by them. The world does not recognize that I am beyond them, that I am eternal.
14. My veil of illusion, my *māyā*, is woven from these strands[2] of nature. It is divine and difficult to grasp. But those who take refuge in me can pass through this veil of illusion.
15. Men who do not take refuge in me do great harm. They are deluded. They are the worst kind of men. The veil of illusion has robbed them of true knowledge, and they descend to demonic behavior.
16. Arjuna, there are four types of virtuous men who do take refuge in me. One comes to me when in distress. There is the seeker of wisdom as well. There is the one who prays to me for wealth and success. And there is the man of knowledge.
17. Among them, the always disciplined man of knowledge is distinguished by his devotion to me alone. I am especially dear to the man of knowledge, and he is dear to me.
18. All of these are noble men, but I think of the man of knowledge

as my very self. For with his disciplined self, he resorts to me as the highest path.

19. At the end of many births, the man of knowledge prays to me, saying to himself, "Kṛṣṇa is all!" Such a great soul is hard to find.
20. All their many desires rob men of their knowledge, and as a result they pray to other gods. They commit themselves to this or that ritual restriction, but it is their own nature that restricts them.
21. I will give unshakable faith to any devotee who wishes to worship god in any form, as long as he worships with fervent faith.
22. When he has gained discipline, he seeks to propitiate his god by means of his faith. He thus obtains his desires from that god, but indeed it is I who have granted them.
23. But such men have little wisdom, and the fruit of their actions is small. Thus those who worship the gods go to the gods, whereas those who are devoted to me come to me.
24. Men who lack insight think that I, the unmanifest one, have become manifest in some particular form. They do not know that higher state of mine which is perfect and unchanging.
25. I am not revealed to everyone. I am veiled by the illusion, the *māyā*, of my yogic power. Deluded as it is, the world does not recognize that indeed I am unborn and unchanging.
26. I know the things of the past and I know the things of the present and, Arjuna, I also know the things of the future. But no one knows me!
27. Arjuna, all beings at birth enter into this grand delusion, because they are deluded[3] by the dualism that arises from loathing and desire.
28. But those who have put an end to their sins, these men who perform acts of merit, they free themselves from the delusions of duality, and they worship me, firm in their vows.

29. Those who restrain themselves, resorting to me for liberation from old age and death, know Brahman completely, and its relation to the self, and the entire world of action.
30. Those who have disciplined their thoughts will know me in all of my aspects—as I relate to creatures, to the gods, and to sacrifice—even at the moment of death!

EIGHT

Arjuna spoke:

1. What is this Brahman? What does it have to do with the self? What has it to do with action, Kṛṣṇa? What does it have to do with beings in general? And what does it have to do with the gods?[1]
2. What exactly is it, and how does it relate to sacrifice,[2] Kṛṣṇa, here in this body? And how exactly are men of self-restraint to know you at the moment of death?

The Blessed One spoke:

3. The supreme Brahman is imperishable. It is said to relate to the self as its inherent nature. It is the creative impulse that causes the origin of all beings. As such, it is also known as action.
4. Brahman relates to beings in general insofar as they come into being and perish by means of it. The individual spirit[3] is that in us which has to do with the gods. And with regard to sacrifice, Arjuna, I am that form of Brahman that dwells in the body.
5. When at the moment of death one abandons the body, holding in mind me alone, one passes on and enters into my state of being. About this there is no doubt.

6. Whatever state of being one holds in mind, when at the moment of death one leaves the body, that is the state that one returns to. Arjuna, that is the state where one has always dwelled.
7. Therefore, at all times you should hold me in memory, and fight! Fix your mind and your attention on me. Without doubt you will come to me.
8. When one meditates with one's mind disciplined by the practice of yoga, pursuing nothing else, then, Arjuna, one comes to that highest divine spirit within us all.
9. One should hold in memory that ancient poet, the lord who is finer indeed than an atom, he who ordains all things, incomprehensible of form, with the radiance of the sun that is beyond this darkness.
10. At the moment of death, one should be disciplined with an unwavering mind, by means of devotion and the power of yoga. One should direct one's breath completely onto the middle point between the brows. By doing so, one attains to this supreme divine spirit.
11. What students of the Vedas call the imperishable, what ascetics who have renounced passion enter into, what those who live the celibate life seek—briefly will I tell you about that place.
12. One should close down all of the doors of the body and keep one's mind within one's heart. One should establish one's breath within the head, and remain fixed in yogic concentration.
13. OM. One should utter the one imperishable syllable that is Brahman. One should hold me firm in memory. When he abandons his body and departs from this life, such a man takes the highest path.[4]
14. For a man who always remembers me, who keeps his thoughts only on me and on nothing else—for an ever-disciplined yogin like this, I am easy to find.
15. Those great souls who have attained the highest perfection come

to me, Arjuna. They do not experience that impermanent home of sorrow which is rebirth.

16. From out of the realm of Brahman all these worlds unfold over and over again. But, Arjuna, whoever comes to me instead will never experience rebirth.
17. When people come to know that a day of Brahman revolves through a thousand ages, and that a night of Brahman lasts a thousand ages also—then they will know truly about days and nights.
18. At the dawn of a day of Brahman all manifest things arise from what is known as the unmanifest, and at the fall of its night they dissolve back into that same unmanifest again.
19. This same vast host of beings arises again and again, and then unwillingly it dissolves at nightfall, and then it all arises again, Arjuna, at the next dawn of day.
20. Beyond all that, there is another state, an eternal unmanifest state that is beyond that unmanifest world. Whereas all beings perish, this one[5] does not die.
21. It is said that this unmanifest being is imperishable, and men say that he is the supreme path. Once they have reached him, they do not return. This is my highest dwelling.
22. But, Arjuna, this highest person can be reached only through devotion to him alone. In him all beings rest and by him all this world is woven.
23. Yogins at the time of death sometimes return to the world, but at other times they do not return. Arjuna, I will tell you about such times.
24. People who know Brahman reach Brahman when they die at the following times: when there is fire, or light, or daytime, or the moonlit fortnight, or the six months of the sun's northern course.
25. But a yogin reaches the light of the moon and returns here when he dies at these times: when there is smoke, or nighttime, or the

dark moonless fortnight, or the six months of the sun's southern course.

26. Indeed, these two courses—the light one and the dark—are thought to be permanent in this world. By means of the one, one does not return to this world. By means of the other, one returns again.
27. By knowing these two paths, Arjuna, a yogin will never become deluded. Therefore, Arjuna, become disciplined at all times in yoga!
28. Whatever reward for merit has been taught in the past regarding the Vedas, sacrifices, austerities, as well as the giving of gifts—the yogin transcends all of this. Having gained this knowledge, the yogin reaches that realm that is both first and last.

NINE

The Blessed One spoke:

1. Now I will teach the greatest of secrets to you, since you do not dispute what I have said so far. When you have understood the wisdom that comes with knowledge, you will be released from misfortune.
2. This is the knowledge of kings, the secret of kings. It is the highest means of purification. It is readily accessible. It conforms to *dharma*. It is easy to accomplish, and it is everlasting!
3. Arjuna, men who do not place their faith in this *dharma* do not return to me. Instead they turn back upon the endless cycle of death and rebirth.
4. I am woven into all this world, yet my form remains unmanifest. All beings find their support in me, whereas I do not depend on them at all.
5. And yet beings also do not find their support in me! Behold the regal force of my yoga! My self brings all beings to life, and supports all beings, but it does not dwell in them.
6. Just as the great wind that goes everywhere dwells eternally in the ether, so all beings dwell in me. Ponder this, Arjuna!

7. At the end of every aeon, all these beings return again to the nature[1] that belongs to me, Arjuna. And at the beginning of the next aeon I send them forth again.
8. Relying on my own nature alone, I send forth again and again this vast host of beings, not by the force of their will but by the force of nature.
9. But these actions do not bind me down. I am seated here, Arjuna, but actually I am like one who sits apart, detached from all of these actions.
10. Nature gives birth to what moves and what does not move—while I oversee it all! Arjuna, the world turns and turns in this way—while this[2] is the cause!
11. Deluded men disregard me when I take on a human body. They do not recognize my higher state, as the great lord of all beings.
12. Their hopes are sheer folly. Their actions are sheer folly. Their wisdom too is sheer folly. They have no insight whatsoever. They surrender themselves to a deluded nature that is full of demons and devils.
13. But great souls surrender instead to a divine nature, Arjuna. They surrender to me! They worship me, thinking of nothing else. Thus they know the eternal source of all beings!
14. Ever singing my praises, ever striving toward me firm in their vows, ever paying homage to me with devotion, ever disciplined—thus do they worship me!
15. And still others make offerings to me with offerings of knowledge. Thus they worship me—I who face in all directions—as having one form, having several, having many forms!
16. I am this ritual. I am this sacrifice. I am the libation for the dead and the healing herb as well. I am this mantra and I am this ghee. I am this ritual fire and its oblation too.
17. I am the father of this world and its mother. I am its guardian

and its grandfather. I am all that is to be known. I am the purifier and the sacred syllable OM. I am the Rigveda and the Sāmaveda and the Yajurveda.

18. I am the way and the support, the lord and the witness. I am your dwelling, your refuge, and your heart's friend. I am the world's origin and its dissolution, its stability, its treasure, its imperishable seed.

19. I myself radiate this heat. I withhold the rain, and then I release it. I am immortality and mortality both. Arjuna, I am being and nonbeing both!

20. Those who study the three Vedas, those who drink the Soma,[3] those who purify themselves of sin—seeking a path to heaven, they all direct their sacrifices to me! They reach the blessed world of Indra, lord of the gods, and in that heaven they partake of the heavenly pleasures of the gods.

21. And having thus enjoyed this heavenly world at length, having exhausted their merit, they return to the world of mortals. In this way those who observe their duties to the three Vedas, those whose desire is desire itself, win only what comes and goes!

22. But those people who devote themselves to me, thinking of nothing else whatsoever, once they have become constant in their discipline—I bring them success and peace.[4]

23. And even the devotees of other gods, who worship in good faith—Arjuna, even if they do not observe the traditional rites, in the end, with their sacrifices, they worship me.

24. For indeed I am the recipient and the lord of all sacrificial offerings, but those who sacrifice to others do not recognize me in my essence, and so they fall from their heavens.

25. Men who offer their vows to the gods go to the gods. Those who offer their vows to the fathers go to the fathers. Those who sacrifice to ghosts go to the ghosts. In the same way, those who worship me come to me.

26. A leaf, or a flower, a fruit, or water, whatever one offers to me with devotion—I accept it, because it is a gift of devotion, because it is offered from the self.
27. Whatever you do—whatever you eat, whatever offering you make, whatever you give, whatever austerity you perform—Arjuna, do it all as an offering to me!
28. In this way you will be freed both from the bonds and also from the fruits of your actions, whether good or bad. Train yourself in the yoga of renunciation. Freed thereby, you will come to me.
29. Among all beings I am always the same. No one is hateful to me. No one is especially dear. But if they worship me with utter devotion, they will be in me, and I will be in them.
30. No matter how badly a man has lived his life, if he worships me and worships nothing else, let him be considered upright and wise, for he has come to recognize what is right.
31. He quickly commits himself to duty and righteousness, and he enters into eternal peace. Arjuna, understand this well: no one who is devoted to me is ever lost to me.
32. For, Arjuna, no matter how low their birth may be—whether they are women, or villagers, or low-caste slaves—those who rely on me all attain to the final goal.
33. How much more is this true, then, for virtuous Brahmins, or devout royal sages! Arjuna, having entered into this fleeting, joyless world, devote yourself to me!
34. To me should your mind be directed, to me your devotion aimed, to me should you make your sacrifices! Pay your homage to me! Disciplining yourself in this way, you will come to me. I will be your final refuge!

TEN

The Blessed One spoke:

1. Once more, Arjuna, listen to my supreme word, which I will now declare to you, since it pleases you to hear it, and since my desire is for your welfare.
2. The hosts of the gods do not know my origins, nor do the great seers, for with regard to the gods and great seers, I myself am their very source!
3. A man who knows that I am unborn and without beginning and the great lord of all worlds is free from all delusions, and among mortals he is released from all evils.
4. Insight, knowledge, freedom from delusion; patience, truth, self-control, and peace; pleasure and pain; coming into being and parting from it; also fear and fearlessness;
5. nonviolence, equanimity, contentment; austerity, generosity, glory and shame—all these conditions that all beings experience, in all of their varieties, arise from me alone.
6. The seven great seers of ancient times and the four ancestors of man all originated in me, born from my mind. All beings in the world are their descendants.

7. Whoever comes to know this power[1] of mine, as it truly is, and yoga as well, will thus come to discipline himself with a form of yoga that is unwavering. There is no doubt about this.
8. I am the origin of all and from me all unfolds. Men of insight who have realized this worship me for this reason, filled as they are with my presence.
9. Their thoughts are focused on me. Their life-breaths go from them to me. They enlighten each other about me and they retell the traditional tales about me. Such things please and comfort them.
10. Because they worship me with unfailing discipline and with love, I give them the yoga of insight by which they will come to me.
11. Out of compassion for them, and with the shining light of knowledge, I destroy that darkness that is born of ignorance. All the while I remain within myself, in my true state.

Arjuna spoke:

12. You are the supreme Brahman, the supreme foundation, and the supreme purifier as well. You are the human spirit, eternal and divine, the unborn primordial god and lord.
13. All the seers say this of you, and the divine sage Nārada too, and Asita Devala, and Vyāsa also. And now you yourself tell me that it is so.
14. All that you have told me, Kṛṣṇa, I accept as true. Indeed, neither the gods nor the demons know, Lord, your manifest form.
15. O supreme Spirit, you alone know yourself by means of your self alone! O source and lord of all beings! O god of gods, O lord of the world!
16. Please explain to me completely the divine powers of the self, the very powers by means of which you dwell in and pervade these worlds.
17. Here I am meditating constantly on you, great yogin! How

should I understand you? And what are the many states of being, Lord, in which I should conceive of you?

18. Kṛṣṇa, tell me more, and in full detail, of your yoga and its powers, for I haven't had enough of listening to the nectar of your words!

The Blessed One spoke:

19. Come, then, and I will tell you about the divine powers of my self, starting with the most important ones. But as for full detail concerning me, Arjuna, there is no end!
20. I am the very self, Arjuna, that resides in the heart of all beings. I am their beginning and their middle and their end.
21. Among the divine sons of Aditi I am Viṣṇu. Among the celestial lights I am the radiant sun. I am lightning among the gods of the storm. And I am the moon among the stars.
22. Among the Vedas I am the Sāmaveda, the book of songs. Among the gods I am Indra, their king. Among the senses I am the mind, and among the sentient I am consciousness.
23. Among the terrifying deities I am the gentle one [Śiva],[2] and among demons and devils I am Kubera, the lord of wealth. Among the bright gods of space I am Agni, god of fire, and among great mountains I am Meru.
24. Arjuna, know that I am the foremost among domestic priests, Bṛhaspati. Among generals I am Skanda, the god of war, and I am also the ocean among the waters.
25. Among the great seers I am Bhṛgu, and among words I am the sacred syllable OM. Among sacrifices I am the chanted prayer. Among mountain ranges I am the Himālaya.
26. Among all trees I am the sacred fig tree, and among the divine seers I am Nārada. Among the celestial musicians I am Citraratha, their chief, and among perfected saints I am Kapila.
27. Among horses, know that I am Indra's stallion, born of immor-

tality. Among elephants I am Indra's elephant, and among all men I am king.

28. Among weapons I am the *vajra*, Indra's thunderbolt, and among milk cows I am the wish-fulfilling cow,[3] and as for procreation I am Kandarpa, the god of love. I am Prince Vāsuki among snakes.

29. Among serpents I am Ananta, the cosmic water snake, and I am also Varuṇa, lord of the gods of the sea. And I am Aryaman, lord of the ancestors, and I am also the lord of the dead, Yama, chief among those who lead to the otherworld.

30. Among demons I am Prahlāda, the pious. Among calendar makers I am time. Among wild beasts I am the lion, their king, and among birds I am Viṣṇu's bird, Garuḍa.

31. Among the things that purify I am the purifying wind. Among men bearing arms I am Rāma.[4] Among sea monsters I am the crocodile, and among rivers indeed I am the Ganges.

32. Arjuna, I am the beginning and the end of all created worlds, and I am their middle as well. Among sciences I am the science of the self, and among those who argue I am the argument.

33. Among syllables I am the syllable A. Among word combinations I am the couple.[5] I am also imperishable time, the creator facing in all directions.

34. And I am death that carries everything away, and also the birth of those who will be born. Among feminine nouns[6] I am Fame and Fortune and Speech; Memory also, and Wisdom and Stability and Patience.

35. Among the Vedic chants I am the high chant. Among the meters I am the *gāyatrī* meter. Among the months I am Mārgaśīrṣa, the first month, and among the seasons I am the flower-bearer, Spring.

36. Among gamblers who cheat I am the game of dice. Among the glorious I am glory. I am the conquest and I am the exertion and I am the courage of the courageous.

37. Among the clan of the Vṛṣṇis I am Kṛṣṇa, among the Pāṇḍavas I am Arjuna. Among the holy hermits I am Vyāsa, and among the ancient poets I am the poet Uśanas.
38. I am the rod of the punishers. I am the policy of scheming politicians. I am also the silence of secret doctrines. And I am the wisdom that wise men know.
39. And beyond that, I am the seed of all beings, Arjuna. Nothing—neither what moves nor what does not move—could exist without me!
40. O Arjuna, there is no end to my divine powers! But I have shown you the extent of my power by using just a few examples.
41. Understand that whatever displays divine power, or great beauty, or enormous vigor, arises from but a small portion of my own glory!
42. But what use is it to you, Arjuna, to know all of this? With one small portion of myself I have propped up this entire world, and still I stand here.

ELEVEN

Arjuna spoke:

1. As a kindness to me, you have explained the sublime secret doctrine concerning the self. Your words have freed me from my delusion.
2. Indeed, O Kṛṣṇa, you whose eyes are like lotus petals and whose greatness is unending—I have heard from you in detail of the arising and the passing away of all beings!
3. I want to see you as you have described yourself, Kṛṣṇa, in your true form, as the lord of the world, for you are the supreme Spirit.
4. If you think that it is possible for me to see you as you really are, lord and master of yoga, then please show your eternal self to me!

The Blessed One spoke:

5. Arjuna, look at the forms that I take, hundreds of them and thousands of them! So many divine forms! So many colors and so many shapes!
6. Look at them all: gods of heaven, gods of light, terrifying gods; the celestial twins and the storm gods. Look at these wonders, Arjuna, so many, never seen before!

7. Look now at this whole world, here in one place, both what moves and what does not move, all of it here within my body! And whatever else you wish to see, Arjuna!
8. But of course you cannot see me with your own eye alone. Here, I give you a divine eye. Now look at my majestic yoga![1]

Saṁjaya spoke:

9. O my king, thus he spoke, Kṛṣṇa, the great lord of yoga, who is also Viṣṇu![2] And thus he unveiled to Arjuna his supreme majestic form.
10. Kṛṣṇa in this form was a great wonder to see, with many mouths and many eyes, with many divine ornaments, and many divine weapons raised up in his arms.
11. Divine also were the garlands and robes that he wore. Divine were the perfumes and ointments. His divinity was an endless profusion of wonders. And in every direction were his many faces turned!
12. If the light of a thousand suns were to suddenly arise in heaven—as at the dawn of a new age—that would be like the radiance of this great soul!
13. There Arjuna saw the entire world, the whole world in all of its infinite manifestations, drawn together as one, in the body of the god of gods.
14. And so, thus seized with wonder, the hair on his body bristling with ecstasy, Arjuna joined his hands together in reverence, bowed his head to the god, and said:

Arjuna spoke:

15. I see all of the gods within your body, O god of gods! I see the whole array of beings—the lord Brahmā sitting on his lotus seat, all of the seers, and the celestial serpents!
16. Countless arms, countless bellies, countless mouths and eyes—I see you everywhere in this infinite variety of forms! I see no end-

ing to you, no middle, and no beginning. You, who are the lord of all things and the form of all things!

17. I see you here, wearing your crown, bearing your mace and discus. I see you full of light, your radiance pouring forth in all directions. I see you everywhere, but it is a sight that is hard to bear. Immeasurable light of flames and fires and suns and lightning!

18. You are the imperishable, the supreme, the goal of all knowledge. You are the world's finest treasure house. You are the unfailing guardian of unchanging *dharma.* Thus I now understand: you are the eternal spirit in man.

19. I now see that you are without beginning or middle or end, that your power is infinite, that your arms are beyond number, that the sun and the moon are your eyes. I now see that your mouth is a blazing sacrificial fire and that your radiance burns up all this world.

20. For you alone pervade this space between heaven and earth and all of the directions within it. The three worlds gaze upon your wondrous and terrible body, Kṛṣṇa, and they tremble!

21. Multitudes of gods enter you. Some of them are terrified. They hold their hands in reverence to you and they sing your praises. Multitudes of seers and perfected sages chant to you in copious rounds of recitation.

22. Terrifying gods and heavenly gods, bright gods, and perfected gods; universal gods, the divine twins, storm gods, and ancestral spirits; hosts of celestial musicians, sprites, demons, and saints—they all look upon you now and are seized with wonder.

23. Kṛṣṇa, when the worlds see this massive form of yours, with its many mouths and eyes, with its many arms and legs and feet, its many bellies and terrible tusks—they look and they tremble, as I do now!

24. I see your body as it touches the clouds, shining a rainbow of colors, your large gaping mouth, your wide flaming eyes. My

inmost self trembles. I cannot find my resolve, Viṣṇu. I cannot find peace.

25. I see your mouths and your wide gaping tusks that look to me like the fires at the end of time. I am disoriented now and can find no shelter. Kṛṣṇa, lord of the gods and the world's repose, have mercy!

26. And now all of those sons of Dhṛtarāṣṭra, together with their host of kings, Bhīṣma, Droṇa, and Karṇa, the son of the charioteer, are here—and our best warriors are here as well.

27. They rush headlong past your gaping, terrifying tusks into your countless mouths. Some of them seem to hang lifeless, caught between your teeth, with their heads crushed.

28. Like the countless river torrents that flow back toward the sea, those heroes in the worlds of men pour into your blazing mouths.

29. Like the moths that rush frantically to the burning flame, and to their destruction, so these worlds rush in a frenzy into your mouths, to their destruction.

30. Viṣṇu,[3] you devour everything, all these worlds, licking at them with your flaming tongues. You fill the whole world with your brilliance. O your terrible flames, how they burn!

31. Tell me, who are you, O lord of such terrible form? Let me pay homage to you. O best of gods, have mercy! I wish to know you as you were in the beginning, because I do not understand your present course.

The Blessed One spoke:

32. I am time, the agent of the world's destruction, now grown old and set in motion to destroy the worlds. Even without you, all of these warriors arrayed in opposing battle-formation will cease to exist!

33. Therefore, rise up and seek your glory! Conquer your enemies and enjoy successful kingship! In fact, I have slain them all already, long ago. Simply be the instrument by my side!

34. Droṇa and Bhīṣma and Jayadratha, and Karṇa as well—and all the other war heroes—have been killed by me already, so now you should kill them. Don't waver! Fight! You will defeat your rivals in this war!

Saṁjaya spoke:

35. Arjuna listened to Kṛṣṇa's words. Trembling beneath his crown, he brought his hands together in homage and bowed, and again he spoke to Kṛṣṇa. He stammered, overwhelmed by fear.

Arjuna spoke:

36. It is fitting, Kṛṣṇa, that the world rejoices and devotes itself to your praise, and that the frightened demons flee in all directions. The hosts of perfected sages also pay homage.
37. And why shouldn't they pay homage to you, great soul—a creator more worthy than Brahmā himself?[4] You are the infinite lord of the gods and the world's resting place. You are the imperishable, both what exists and what does not exist, and beyond them both.
38. You are the first among all gods, the ancient spirit. You are the final resting place of all things. You are both the knower and the known and the world's supreme foundation. Kṛṣṇa, you reach everywhere into all of this world!
39. You are the god of the wind, and you are death. You are fire, and the god of the waters and of the moon. You are the Lord of Creation, the Grandfather of Creation. Homage to you, a thousand homages to you! And again homage to you!
40. Homage before you and homage behind you, let there be homage to you, the all, on all sides! O Kṛṣṇa, endless hero, your striving power is unmeasured. You embrace all of it, and indeed you are all of it!
41. Whatever I may have said impulsively, thinking "This is my friend," addressing you "Hello Kṛṣṇa, hello Yādava, hello my

friend!" unaware as I was of your true greatness, whether out of carelessness or affection,

42. and if while joking I have said something offensive, while relaxing or resting or sitting or eating with you—whether alone or publicly—immeasurable Kṛṣṇa, I seek your forgiveness.
43. You are the Father of the world of the things that move and the things that do not move. You are the world's guru, the best and most revered. Kṛṣṇa, there is no one equal to you in the three worlds—so how could there be one greater?
44. Therefore, I bow down and I prostrate this body. I seek grace from you, a lord to be revered above all others. Like a father to a son, like a friend to a friend, like a lover to a loved one—please, God, bear with me!
45. I have seen what no one else has seen before, and I am exhilarated, but my mind is shaken with fear. Kṛṣṇa, please show me once again that body that I know so well. Lord of the gods, the world's refuge, be gracious!
46. I wish to see you again as you used to be, wearing your crown, bearing your mace and your discus. O Kṛṣṇa of the thousand arms, true body of all this world, return to that four-armed body that I know so well![5]

The Blessed One spoke:

47. As a kindness to you, Arjuna, and as an expression of my yogic power, I have revealed my supreme form to you. It is radiant, universal, endless, and primordial, and with the exception of you alone, no one has seen it before.
48. I can be seen in this form in the world of men only by you, Arjuna, hero of the Kurus! The Vedas will not help, nor will sacrifices, nor will much studying or gift-giving. The performance of ritual will not help, nor will terrible austerities!

49. Do not waver. Do not be confused. Now you have seen this my terrifying form—for such it is! But let go of this fear. Put your mind at ease. Look again at this body of mine that you know so well.

Saṁjaya spoke:

50. Kṛṣṇa spoke these words to Arjuna and revealed himself again in his familiar form. And by returning to this gentle form again, the great soul gave that frightened man a moment to regain his breath.

Arjuna spoke:

51. Kṛṣṇa, once again I can see this human, gentle form of yours. Now I am settled down, in control of my thoughts again. I am back to my normal state.

The Blessed One spoke:

52. The gods themselves constantly yearn for a view of this body of mine that you have now seen. Indeed, it is a body that is difficult to look upon.
53. I will not be seen in this form as you have now seen me, neither through the study of the Vedas, nor through the practice of austerities. Nor is gift-giving of any use. Nor is sacrifice.
54. It is only through devotion, *bhakti*, that I can be known in this way. Only through devotion to me alone can I be known and seen as I really am and entered into.
55. Whoever performs his actions for my sake, whoever makes me his highest goal, whoever devotes himself to me, without attachment and without hostility toward anyone—Arjuna, such a man comes to me.

TWELVE

Arjuna spoke:

1. There are some who are constantly disciplined, devotees who worship you. There are others who devote themselves to the imperishable, the unmanifest. Who among them have the best knowledge of yoga?

The Blessed One spoke:

2. I consider them to be the best disciplined who focus their minds on me, who, constant in their discipline, worship me with the greatest faith.
3. But those who worship the imperishable, the unmanifest, which is beyond words, which is found everywhere and is inconceivable, sublime on the mountaintop, unmoving and firm,
4. who have gained complete control over the senses and equanimity toward all beings, rejoicing in the welfare of all beings, they also attain to me.
5. There is greater distress for those who have set their thoughts on the unmanifest, because it is difficult for those who are embodied to reach a goal that is itself unmanifest.

6. But those who surrender all of their actions to me and who are focused on me alone, who meditate on me with yoga, and worship me,
7. I will lift them up out of the ocean of the cycle of death and rebirth, Arjuna, once they have set their thoughts on me.
8. Keep your mind fixed on me. Make your intelligence enter into me. Thus you will come to dwell in me, without question.
9. But if you cannot concentrate your thoughts firmly on me, then, Arjuna, try to reach me through the diligent practice of yoga.
10. And if you are incapable of this sort of practice, then make it your goal to perform action for my sake. If you perform your ritual and social actions for my sake, you will find success!
11. And if you are unable to do even that, then simply resort to me in yoga. Renounce the fruit of all of your actions. Restrain yourself, and act!
12. For in fact wisdom is better than practice, and meditation is better than wisdom. Abandoning the fruit of action is better than meditation, for from this abandonment peace follows immediately.
13. Let there be no hatred in you. Offer friendship and compassion to all living things. Give up thoughts of "I" and "mine." Accept both pleasure and sorrow alike, and endure all things with patience.
14. The yogin who is always content and self-restrained and firm in his resolve, and who directs his mind and his awareness upon me—he is my devotee, and he is dear to me.
15. The world does not tremble in fear before him, nor does he tremble in fear before the world. He has freed himself from the disturbances of joy or impatience or fear, and so he is dear to me.
16. He is indifferent to circumstance. He is pure and capable. He is a detached witness, untroubled by events. He does not initiate new engagements—he is my devotee, and he is dear to me.

17. He does not delight in things, nor does he loathe them. He knows neither anguish nor longing. Indifferent to good fortune and to bad fortune alike, he is a man of devotion, and he is dear to me.
18. In the presence of an enemy or a friend, he is impartial to both, just as he is in the presence of honor or dishonor, or heat or cold, or pleasure or sorrow. He is impartial and unattached.
19. A silent sage for whom blame and praise are the same, content with whatever happens, homeless but firm in his mind, he is a man of devotion, and he is dear to me.
20. In fact, all who worship this divine nectar of *dharma* that I have now declared to you, all who have placed their faith in this teaching, all such devotees for whom I am the supreme goal are dear to me—even more!

THIRTEEN

The Blessed One spoke:

1. Arjuna, this body of yours is known as the field, and one who knows it as such is called the knower of the field. This is what those who have studied this doctrine say.
2. And know also, Arjuna, that in all fields I alone am the knower of the field. Knowledge of both of these—the field and the knower of the field—is what I consider true knowledge.
3. Hear from me briefly what this field is, and what its features and variations are, and where it comes from, and who the knower of the field is, and what his powers are.
4. It has been sung in many ways by the ancient seers and in various meters and on many occasions, and in the words of the verses, the *sūtras*, on Brahman. It has been extensively argued and it has now become settled doctrine.
5. There are the gross elements, the ego-sense, consciousness, unmanifest nature, the eleven senses, and the five sense realms.
6. There are desire and loathing, pleasure and pain, the physical body, awareness, steadfastness: this is a brief description of the field and its manifestations.

7. Knowledge is said to consist in the absence of pride and deceit, of nonviolence and patience and upright honesty, of service to one's teacher, purity, stability, and self-control,
8. dispassion with regard to sense objects, and the absence of an ego-sense. There should also be an accurate perception of the misfortunes that inevitably come with birth and death, and old age and disease and sorrow,
9. the absence of attachment or affection toward a son or a wife or a home, and all the rest; the constant practice of equanimity, whether events are wished for or not wished for,
10. and there should be undeviating devotion, along with yoga focused on me alone, a preference for solitary places, and a distaste for large crowds.
11. Finally, there should be constant attention to knowledge of the self, and a perception of the purpose of the knowledge of reality—all of this is called true knowledge. What differs from this is just ignorance.
12. I will now teach you what you should know. Once one knows this, one attains immortality. It is Brahman, supreme and without beginning. It is said to be neither being nor nonbeing.
13. Its hands and feet are everywhere, its eyes and heads and faces everywhere. Its ears are everywhere. It stands still, covering everything in the world.
14. It appears to have all of the sense qualities, and yet it does not have sense organs. It is detached, and yet it supports all things. It has no qualities,[1] and yet it enjoys them all.
15. It is at once outside and inside all creatures. It moves and it does not move. It cannot be explained because it is too subtle. It is both far away and very near.
16. It is undivided and indivisible, and yet it appears to be divided among all beings. It is understood to be the support of all beings, and yet it devours them and brings them forth again.

17. It is the light of lights, and it is said to be beyond darkness. It is knowledge, and the object of knowledge, and the goal of knowledge. It is set firmly in the heart of all things.
18. Thus I have explained briefly the field, and knowledge of the field, and the goal of that knowledge. My devotee understands this and enters into my essence.
19. Material nature and the spirit of man[2] are both without beginning—know this doctrine! And know also that their modifications and qualities, the *guṇa*s, arise within the natural world.
20. Nature is said to be the cause of action insofar as actions have effects and instruments and agents. But insofar as there is experience of pleasure and pain, the cause of action is said to be the spirit in man.
21. For the human spirit dwells within nature and experiences the qualities that arise from nature. Its attachment to these qualities is the cause of birth in either good wombs or bad ones.
22. The great lord, also said to be the supreme soul, is also known as the human spirit when it dwells in the body: he is the one who experiences the world, and supports it, and observes it, and consents to it.
23. Whoever knows well the human spirit and nature, with its qualities—no matter what his present condition is—he is not reborn again.
24. By meditating on the self, some men see the self, by means of the self. Others do so by means of the practice, the yoga, of Sāṁkhya reasoning, and still others by means of the yoga of action.
25. But others, not knowing these doctrines, nevertheless hear them from others and revere them. They take the traditional revelation of the Vedas as their guide, and so they too cross beyond death.
26. Any being that is born, whether inanimate or animate, is born from the union of the field and the knower of the field. Arjuna, you should know this doctrine!

27. Whoever is able to see in all beings the supreme lord standing there, among those who are dying while he himself does not die—he sees things as they are!
28. For when he sees the lord dwelling everywhere, and everywhere the same, he himself does not harm the self in others. Thus he goes to the highest goal.
29. Whoever sees that all actions are performed everywhere by nature alone, and that the self is not the agent—he sees things as they are!
30. When he recognizes the oneness that dwells within the diversity of all beings, and that from this all beings disperse—then he unites with Brahman.
31. Because it has no beginning, because it has no real properties, this supreme self is eternal and unchanging. Arjuna, though it dwells in the body, it does not act, nor is it defiled by action.
32. Just as all-pervading space—so subtle!—is not defiled by the things that dwell in it, so the self that pervades the body is not defiled by it.
33. Arjuna, just as only one sun illuminates this entire world, so the lord of the field alone illuminates this entire field.
34. Those who know the difference between the field and the knower of the field, and who know, with the eye of knowledge, this doctrine concerning the liberation of all beings from nature—they go to the highest!

FOURTEEN

The Blessed One spoke:

1. I will now declare still more concerning this highest knowledge, the supreme among all doctrines. Knowing it, all of the holy men have gone from this world to highest perfection.
2. When they rely on this knowledge and have come to have the same virtues and duties that I have, when a world cycle arises they are not reborn, and they are not disturbed when one collapses.
3. The great Brahman is my womb. I plant my seed in it. The origin of all beings originates from this, Arjuna!
4. For the forms that originate within all of the wombs of the world, Arjuna, the great Brahman is their womb, and I am the Father who gives the seed.
5. Clarity, passion, dark inertia. These are the qualities[1] that originate from nature. Arjuna, they bind the unchanging embodied self within a body.
6. Among these, clarity because it is untainted radiates light and good health. It binds one through attachment to pleasure, and through attachment to knowledge.

7. Passion is essentially desire. Know that it arises from attachment to craving. Arjuna, it binds the embodied soul through attachment to action.
8. And know that dark inertia is born of ignorance. It deludes all embodied souls. It binds the soul through carelessness, laziness, and sleep.
9. Clarity induces attachment to pleasure, and passion to action, Arjuna. But dark inertia obscures knowledge and induces attachment to carelessness.
10. Clarity increases by overcoming passion and dark inertia. Passion increases by overcoming clarity and dark inertia, and dark inertia increases by overcoming clarity and passion.
11. When the light that is knowledge appears in all of the gateways of the body, then one will know that clarity has increased.
12. Greed, strenuous effort, endless involvement in action, restlessness, longing—Arjuna, these arise when passion increases.
13. And, Arjuna, when dark inertia increases, then these things arise—obscurity, lack of effort, carelessness, and finally delusion.
14. If an embodied soul dies at a moment when clarity prevails, then he attains to the untainted worlds of those who know this highest truth.
15. But if one dies while in a state of passion, one is reborn among those who are attached to action. And if one dies while in a state of dark inertia, one is reborn in wombs of the deluded.
16. It is said that the fruit of an action that is done well consists of clarity and purity, and that the fruit of passion is suffering, and that the fruit of dark inertia is ignorance.
17. Wisdom is born from clarity, just as greed is born from passion, and carelessness and delusion are born from dark inertia.
18. Those who stand firm in clarity rise upward. Those who are

passionate stand in the middle of things. Those who incline to dark inertia go downward, dwelling in the lowest conditions of nature.

19. When one becomes clear in one's vision and recognizes that there is no agent other than the conditions of nature, the *guṇas*, and when one knows what is higher than any of these conditions, then one enters into my state.
20. When the embodied soul transcends these three conditions of nature that are the origins of the body, then he is freed from the sorrows that accompany birth and death and old age, and he attains immortality.

Arjuna spoke:

21. Lord, what are the signs that identify the man who has transcended these three conditions? How does he go about in the world? And how does he get beyond these three conditions?

The Blessed One spoke:

22. Arjuna, as for illumination and activity and even delusion—he does not experience aversion when they arise, nor does he experience longing when they disappear.
23. Sitting apart like a witness, he is not disturbed by the conditions of nature. He merely thinks to himself, "These conditions, these *guṇas*, unfold." He stands firm. He is untroubled.
24. He stays within himself, indifferent to sorrow and pleasure. A clod of earth, a rock, a piece of gold—they are all the same to him! He is wise for whom a friend and a stranger are both alike, for whom blame and praise of himself are alike!
25. Indifferent to both honor and disgrace, impartial to allies and enemies alike, renouncing all intrigues, such a man is said to have transcended the conditions of nature.

26. The man who worships me with the undeviating yoga of devotion, and who has transcended these conditions of nature, is ready to become Brahman.
27. For I am the foundation of Brahman, of the immortal and the imperishable, and of the eternal law, *dharma*, and of absolute bliss!

FIFTEEN

The Blessed One spoke:

1. There is an eternal fig tree, with its roots above and its branches below, and they say that the Vedic hymns are its leaves. Whoever knows this tree indeed knows the Vedas.
2. First downward and then upward spread its branches. They are nourished by the conditions of nature. Its sprouts are the sense objects, and below are its roots, which extend down into the world of men, all bound up with their actions.
3. Its form cannot be perceived here as it really is—neither its end nor its beginning nor its foundation. This tree with its fully grown roots—one should cut it down with the strong ax of detachment![1]
4. And then one should seek out that place where those have gone who do not return again, saying, "I resort to that primordial person from whom the ancient process of creation has flowed forth."
5. To that eternal place go the undeluded, those who have neither pride nor confusion, who have overcome the harmful effects of attachment. They dwell constantly on what relates to the self.

They extinguish desire. They free themselves from the dualities that are experienced as pleasure and pain.

6. Neither the sun nor the moon, nor fire, illuminates that place that they go to who do not return again. That place is my highest dwelling.
7. In the world of the living, one small portion of me becomes a living being. It remains eternal. It draws to itself the things of nature—the five sense organs and the mind.
8. When the lord takes on a body, or when he leaves one behind, he takes these things away with him when he goes, just as the wind carries fragrances away from their source.
9. Hearing and sight and touch and taste and smell—the lord governs these things and the mind as well. Indeed, he savors sense objects.
10. But the deluded do not recognize him as he leaves a body, or as he dwells in one, or as he experiences the body, engaged as it is in the conditions of nature. But those who have the eye of knowledge see him there!
11. Yogins who exert themselves see that he is present within themselves. But no matter how much they exert themselves, the thoughtless do not see him, because they have not yet perfected themselves.
12. The radiance that belongs to the sun which illuminates the entire world, and that radiance that is in the moon and in fire—know that all this radiance is mine!
13. I penetrate the earth, and I sustain all beings with my power. And I nourish all the plants of the world. And I have become Soma, whose essence is nectar!
14. I am the fire that dwells in all men, and I dwell in the body of all that have breath. Joined together with the exhalations and the inhalations of the breath, I cook and digest the four kinds of food.

15. I have also entered into the heart of all beings. From me come memory and knowledge and the give-and-take of debate. I am the very thing in the Vedas that is worth knowing. I am the author of the Vedānta,[2] and I am the knower of the Vedas.
16. There are two divine persons in the world. One is perishable and the other is imperishable. The perishable consists of all beings whatsoever. The imperishable is called what dwells on the mountaintop.
17. But there is another beside these two, the highest spirit, called the supreme self. He is the eternal lord who enters and supports the three worlds.
18. Since I transcend the perishable, and since I am higher than the imperishable, so in the world and in the Veda I am celebrated as the highest spirit.
19. Whoever without delusion thus knows me as the highest spirit knows everything! Arjuna, he worships me with his entire being.
20. Thus have I taught you this most secret doctrine. Blameless Arjuna, once one has become awakened to this doctrine, then one will have become awakened! And all that one has needed to do will have been done!

SIXTEEN

The Blessed One spoke:

1. Fearlessness, purity of character; steadfastness in the yoga of knowledge; gift-giving, self-control, and sacrifice; study of the Vedas and austerity and honesty;
2. nonviolence and truth and no anger; renunciation and peacefulness and no slander; compassion for all beings and no greed; gentleness and modesty and no fickleness;
3. radiance, patience, resolve, purity; no deception and no exaggerated pride—Arjuna, these are the qualities of a man who has been born into a divine destiny.
4. But, Arjuna, the qualities of a man born into a demonic destiny are: hypocrisy, arrogance, exaggerated pride, anger, harsh speech, and ignorance.
5. Divine destiny leads to release. Demonic destiny leads to bondage. But do not worry, Arjuna. You are born into a divine destiny.
6. There are two kinds of creation in this world: the divine and the demonic. I have spoken of the divine at length. Arjuna, hear now from me of the demonic.

7. Demonic people do not distinguish between activity and the cessation of activity. You will not find purity, or the observance of custom, or truth in them.
8. They say that the world has no reality, no religious basis, no god. They deny that the world arises through mutual causation. If not caused by this, then by what else? They say that the world is driven by desire.[1]
9. Stubbornly maintaining this view, these lost souls[2] with so little insight rise up and seize power through terrible acts of violence, wretched people intent on destroying the world.
10. They surrender themselves to insatiable desire. They are intoxicated by their own hypocrisy and pride. They are seized by delusion, and so they themselves seize upon false ideas. They engage in practices that pollute them.
11. They devote themselves to anxiety beyond measure, which ends only when they die. They have convinced themselves that this is all that life amounts to, and so their greatest ambition is to satisfy their desires.
12. Hope, with its hundred snares, binds them, and desire and anger preoccupy them. They strive for vast hoards of wealth by illegal means in order to fulfill their vain desires.
13. "I have gotten this much today, and next I will get this wish fulfilled too. This wealth is mine, and that is too. And I'll have more in the future.
14. I have killed this enemy today, and I will kill others as well. I am the lord here. I enjoy myself. I am successful, powerful, and happy!
15. I am rich and well-born. Who else can compare with me? I will perform the sacrifices. I will give to the poor. I will enjoy myself!" This is how such ignorant fools talk!
16. Distracted by their many worries, they are caught in the web of

delusion. Obsessed with satisfying their desires, they fall headlong into a polluted hell.

17. Self-absorbed, stubborn, intoxicated with wealth and pride, they perform their sacrifices in name only, dishonestly, ignoring the traditional obligations.

18. Egotism, violence, pride, desire, and anger—they resort to these, and in their envy they hate me, both in their own and in all other bodies.

19. In the endless rounds of rebirth, I cast these vile, hateful, bloodthirsty, these lowest of men, over and over again into demonic wombs.

20. And deluded they enter, in birth after birth, into a demonic womb. Arjuna, they do not ever reach me. In this way they take the lowest path.

21. This is the destruction of the self. This is the threefold gate of hell. Desire, anger, and greed. One should abandon these three.

22. But, Arjuna, a man who is released from these three gates of hell engages in what is good for the self. In this way he takes the highest path.

23. If a man neglects the injunctions of tradition,[3] and behaves according to the demands of his own desires, he will not gain success or happiness or the highest path.

24. Therefore, let traditional law be your authority in deciding what is right to do and what is not. Know what is taught in the law books. You should perform here the actions that you are obliged to perform.

SEVENTEEN

Arjuna spoke:

1. There are those who neglect the injunctions of tradition, yet they faithfully perform sacrifices nevertheless. Kṛṣṇa, what is their condition? Is it clarity, or passion, or dark inertia?

The Blessed One spoke:

2. Among embodied souls there are three kinds of faith. This arises from each one's own nature. Thus there is the quality of clarity, and of passion, and of inertia. Listen now to what I say about faith.
3. Each man's faith conforms to his true nature. Arjuna, a man is made up of his faith. What he puts his faith in is what he himself is.
4. Men of clarity offer sacrifices to the gods. Men of passion sacrifice to spirits and demons. And those others, men of darkness, sacrifice to the dead and to ghosts.
5. Some men practice horrible austerities that are not ordained by tradition. They are motivated by hypocrisy and egotism. They are driven by the force of desire and passion.
6. They recklessly starve the cluster of elements that reside in the

body. And they starve me as well, the one who dwells within the body. Know that their resolve is demonic.

7. Also the kinds of food that men enjoy are of three kinds. Likewise also are their sacrifices and their austerities and their gifts. Hear how these are to be classified.
8. Foods that men of clarity prefer increase one's life span, strength, courage, good health, contentment, and pleasure. Such foods are tasty, mild, firm, and easy to digest.
9. A man of passion desires foods that are pungent, sour, salty, very hot, sharp, dry, or burning. Such foods cause discomfort and pain and indigestion.
10. The food that is preferred by men of dark inertia is spoiled, tasteless, putrid, or stale—such as leftovers or food that is unfit for sacrifice.
11. A sacrifice is *sāttvika* and is characterized by clarity, when it is offered with attention to the traditional injunctions, and by men who have no desire for rewards. They concentrate their minds, thinking only "This sacrifice must be performed."
12. Arjuna, know that a sacrifice is *rājasa* and is characterized by passion, when it is performed in order to gain some reward, or when it is offered insincerely.
13. A sacrifice is said to be *tāmasa* and characterized by dark inertia, when it is performed without faith, with no regard for the traditional injunctions, when the food offerings are neglected, mantras are not recited, and sacrificial fees are not paid.
14. To honor the gods, and the twice-born Brahmins, and gurus and the wise, and to be pure and honest and chaste and nonviolent—this is called the austerity of the body.
15. Words that do not agitate, words that are true and pleasing and kind—as well as the daily practice of Vedic recitations—these are called the austerity of speech.

16. Serenity of mind, gentleness, meditative silence, self-control, the purification of one's emotions—these are called the austerity of the mind.
17. This threefold austerity is considered to be *sāttvika.* It is performed with the highest faith by men who have no desire for reward for their actions.
18. But austerity that is performed with desire for the respect, honor, reverence that austerity wins, such austerity is performed insincerely. It is called *rājasa.* It is austerity dominated by passion. It is wavering and unstable.
19. When austerity is performed because of deluded ideas, or as a form of self-mortification, or as a means of destroying someone else—it is considered to be *tāmasa* and ruled by dark inertia.
20. As for gift-giving, when it is given with the thought that it ought to be given, when given to one who is unable to reciprocate, when given at the proper place and time, and to a worthy person, tradition calls it giving from the state of clarity. It is *sāttvika.*
21. But when a gift is given in order to get a gift in return, or with consideration of reward, or if it is given reluctantly, tradition calls it giving from the state of passion. It is *rājasa.*
22. When a gift is given at an inappropriate place and time, and to people who are not worthy, when it is given with disrespect and contempt—then it is known as giving from the state of darkness. It is *tāmasa.*
23. OM TAT SAT![1] This is preserved by tradition as the threefold explanation of Brahman. By means of it, in the ancient days, the Brahmin priests, the Vedas, and the sacrifices were established.
24. Therefore, those who teach the doctrine of Brahman always recite OM before performing sacrifices, giving gifts, and practicing austerities—as required by tradition.

25. Those who seek liberation recite TAT ["that"] when they perform the various acts of sacrifice, and austerity, and gift-giving—doing so without any concern for rewards.
26. The word SAT is used in the sense "true" and also in the sense "good." Arjuna, it is also used to refer to actions that are praiseworthy.
27. With regard to sacrifice and austerity and gift-giving, steadfastness in these activities is said to be SAT—good and true. And all action that is performed for such purposes is called SAT.
28. But whatever is offered or given without faith, or whatever austerity is performed without faith—it is called ASAT ["false, unworthy"], Arjuna, because both in this world and in the next it amounts to nothing.

EIGHTEEN

Arjuna spoke:

1. Kṛṣṇa, I want to know the truth about renunciation, and about abandonment also, and what the difference between them is.[1]

The Blessed One spoke:

2. The ancient poets understand that renunciation is the giving up of acts of desire, whereas the learned say that abandonment is the giving up of the fruit of all actions.
3. Some men of insight say that action should be abandoned because it is harmful. But others say that acts of sacrifice and gift-giving and austerity should not be abandoned.
4. Hear my judgment on the matter of abandonment, Arjuna, O tiger among men. Abandonment is known by tradition to be threefold.
5. Works of sacrifice, of gift-giving, of austerity, should not be abandoned. In fact, they should be performed. Sacrifice, gift-giving, austerity—these things purify men of insight.
6. But while such actions should be performed, one should aban-

don attachment to them as well as their fruit. Arjuna, this is my final judgment on this!

7. To abandon an action that is obligatory is not acceptable. To abandon such action out of confusion is recognized by tradition as an act of darkness.
8. Anyone who would abandon an action thinking that it causes pain to others, or out of fear of harm to his own body, does so from a passionate, a *rājasa*, point of view. He will not gain any reward from the abandonment of such things.
9. When an action that is required by custom is performed only because it should be performed, Arjuna, while one abandons attachment to it as well as its fruit, that kind of abandonment is thought to be *sāttvika*, rooted in clarity.
10. One who abandons in this way does not dislike unpleasant actions, nor is he attached to pleasant action. He is filled with clarity, and he is wise, and he has severed himself from doubt.
11. In fact, it is impossible for one who is still in a body to give up action completely. But one who abandons in this way is able to give up the fruits of his actions.
12. At the moment of death, those who have not abandoned the fruits of their action must confront them. These are of three kinds: the desirable, the undesirable, and the mixed. But this is not the case for true *saṁnyāsins.*
13. Arjuna, know that in the teachings of the Sāṃkhya school there are said to be five causes that lead to success in all actions:
14. the material basis or the body; the agent; the instruments of various kinds; the different kinds of exertion; divine fate is the fifth.
15. Whatever action a man undertakes, with the body or speech or the mind,[2] whether lawful or not, these five are the causes.
16. Since this is the case, anyone who regards himself alone as the agent has only partial insight. Confused in his thinking, he does not see at all.

17. A man who has no sense of egotism, and whose awareness is not clouded by attachment, does not really kill, nor is he bound—even if he must kill all of these people!
18. The impulse to action is threefold: it involves knowledge, the object of knowledge, and the knower. And action itself is threefold: it involves an instrument, the act itself, and an agent.
19. The Sāṁkhya doctrine of the three conditions of nature teaches that knowledge, action, and agent are also each threefold, depending on the three conditions. Concerning these, listen further:
20. that knowledge which is rooted in the condition of clarity sees the one unchanging reality that resides in all beings, divided among them and yet not divided. It is important to understand this!
21. Knowledge that is rooted in the condition of passion sees many conditions among all beings, constantly changing, one thing after another.
22. If one's mind is focused completely on only one insignificant task, without considering causes, and without having genuine purpose in it, such knowledge is understood to be conditioned by inertia.
23. An action that is required by tradition and performed by a man who has no interest in its result, without passion or hatred and without attachment—such an action is said to be rooted in clarity.
24. When an action is performed by a man who is driven by desire, or by one who is driven by egotism, involving too much effort—it is held to be rooted in passion.
25. When an action is initiated out of delusion, without regard for its consequences, or for the destruction and violence involved, or merely for one's manly virtue—that action is rooted in dark inertia.
26. The agent who is devoted to liberation, who prefers not to talk about himself, who is determined and vigorous, and unchanged by success or failure—he is rooted in clarity.

27. An intensely passionate man who is eager for the fruits of his actions, who is greedy and violent and impure, who is consumed by his joys and his griefs—he is an agent rooted in passion.
28. On the other hand, an agent is said to be rooted in dark inertia when he is undisciplined, uncivilized, and vulgar, arrogant, dishonest, lazy, depressed, procrastinating.
29. Arjuna, listen: the classification of intelligence and of resolve according to the conditions of nature is also threefold. I will explain each of them to you fully and in detail.
30. That intelligence which knows what activity is and what its cessation is, what is obligatory and what is not, what is fear and what is fearlessness, as well as what is bondage and what is liberation—Arjuna, that insight is rooted in clarity.
31. That intelligence which incorrectly perceives what is lawful duty and what is not, what is obligatory and what is not—Arjuna, that insight is rooted in passion.
32. And that intelligence which supposes—immersed as it is in darkness—that lawlessness[3] is lawful duty, *dharma*, and which imagines everything to be exactly what it is not—such intelligence is buried in darkness.
33. That resolve by means of which one controls the activities of the mind and the breath and the senses as well, that resolve which is practiced with unwavering yoga—that resolve, Arjuna, is based on clarity.
34. But when one tries to attend to one's duties, desires, and ambitions with a resolve that is too attached to them, and when one worries too much about the results—Arjuna, that resolve is based on passion.
35. And that resolve by means of which the complete fool clings fast to sleep and fear and pain and depression and drunkenness—Arjuna, we call that the resolve of darkness.
36. But now listen to me, Arjuna. That happiness is also threefold

wherein one comes to rest through long practice and comes also to the end of suffering.

37. That which at first seems like poison but which in the end is like nectar—such happiness is rooted in clarity and arises from the peace that comes from insight into the self.

38. And that which arises from contact between the senses and sense objects and which at first seems like nectar but in the end is like poison—according to tradition, that sort of happiness is rooted in passion.

39. And that happiness which in its beginning and in its conclusion is mere self-delusion arising from sleep, or sluggishness, or negligence—that is held to be rooted in dark inertia.

40. There is no one on earth or among the gods in heaven who could be free from the three conditions of nature.

41. Arjuna, Brahmins, and warriors, and villagers, and slaves—they all have obligatory caste duties that are distinguished by the qualities that arise from their innate nature.

42. Serenity, self-control, austerity, purity, patience, honesty, as well as knowledge and discrimination, and religious faith—these are the caste duties of a Brahmin, which arise from a Brahmin's nature.

43. Heroism, energy, resolve, skill, and also the refusal to retreat in battle, generosity, and ruling with authority—these are the caste duties of a warrior, which arise from a warrior's nature.

44. Farming, cattle-herding, and trade are the caste duties of a villager, which arise from his nature. And service is the caste duty of a slave, which arises from the nature of a slave.

45. A man achieves success when he is content in doing the work that is his own. Hear how one who is content in doing his own caste duty achieves success!

46. That man finds success in his caste duty when he worships the one who pervades this entire world, the one from whom everything here unfolds.

47. It is better to perform one's own caste duty poorly than to perform another's well. By performing action that conforms to one's own nature, one does not accumulate guilt.
48. Arjuna, one should not give up the work that one is born to do, even if it is harmful. For harm accompanies all of our involvements, just as smoke accompanies fire.
49. One achieves that highest form of perfection beyond action through renunciation.[4] Then one's consciousness remains unattached at all times. One's longings are gone. One has conquered oneself.
50. I will show you how the man who has attained this perfection also attains to Brahman. Briefly, this is the highest culmination of knowledge.
51. Disciplined by a purified awareness, he restrains himself with firm resolve. He abandons sense objects, sounds, and all the rest. He casts off both passion and hatred.
52. He cultivates solitude, and he eats lightly. He is restrained in speech, in body, and in mind. He devotes himself constantly to yoga and meditation. He rests upon dispassion.
53. He has freed himself from egotism, force, pride, desire, and anger, and also from possessiveness. Selfless and serene, he has prepared himself to become Brahman.
54. And having become Brahman and at peace within himself, he does not grieve, he does not desire. The same toward all beings, he attains supreme devotion to me.
55. Through devotion he comes to recognize me, how vast I am and who I truly am. Then, since he knows me as I truly am, he immediately enters into me.
56. Nevertheless, even as he resorts to me, he continues to perform all the actions that he is obliged to do. By my grace[5] he reaches this eternal imperishable place.
57. In your mind keep me as your focus, and surrender all of your

actions to me. Rely on the yoga of insight. Keep your thoughts always fixed on me.

58. With your thoughts on me, you will be able, by my grace, to overcome all difficulty. But if, in your egotism, you will not listen, then you will perish.
59. If egotism leads you to think "I will not fight," your resolve will be useless. Nature itself, *prakṛti*, will compel you in any case.
60. Arjuna, you are bound by your own action, which arises from your very nature. You will do unwillingly the very thing that you wish not to do. This is delusion!
61. The lord is present in all beings. Arjuna, he dwells in the territory of the heart. With his magical power, his *māyā*, he makes all things revolve like the paddles of a watermill.
62. Go to him as your refuge, Arjuna, with your whole being! By his grace you will reach that eternal place, that supreme peace!
63. Such is the wisdom that I have taught you, the most secret of secrets! Consider it fully. And then do what you wish.
64. Listen once more to this my final doctrine, the most secret of all secrets! My love for you is firm. Thus I will tell you what is good for you.
65. Direct your mind to me. Direct your devotion to me. Make your sacrifices to me. Give me your homage. Thus you will come to me. I promise this to you truly, for you are dear to me!
66. Surrender all of your caste duties to me. Come to me as your only refuge. I will set you free from all evil. Do not worry!
67. You must not speak of this to anyone who does not practice austerity or devotion, or to anyone who does not want to hear it, or to anyone who would dispute it.
68. But whoever reveals this highest secret doctrine to those who are devoted to me, and who gives me his utmost devotion—without fail, he will come to me.
69. No one does more precious service to me than this one, among

all men, nor will there ever be any other man on earth more precious to me!

70. And whoever studies and memorizes our dialogue on sacred duty, Arjuna, I consider him to have worshipped me with a sacrifice that is wisdom.
71. And a man who simply listens with faith and without disputing will also be set free, and will attain to the luminous worlds of the meritorious.
72. Have you listened to this doctrine with your mind fully focused on it alone? Arjuna, has this delusion born of ignorance departed from you?

Arjuna spoke:

73. It has departed, Kṛṣṇa. And by your grace my memory has returned. I am firm now. All my doubts are gone. I will do as you say.

Saṁjaya spoke:

74. Thus I have heard this astonishing dialogue that makes the hair stand on end, the discourse between Kṛṣṇa and the great soul Arjuna.
75. I have heard this supreme secret doctrine by the grace of Vyāsa, this doctrine of yoga, exactly as it was taught by Kṛṣṇa, the lord of yoga, himself.
76. O king, I remember, I memorize, this astonishing auspicious discourse between Kṛṣṇa and Arjuna. And time after time it thrills me!
77. And I remember, I memorize also, that wonderfully beautiful form that Kṛṣṇa wears. My king, it fills me with wonder. And again and again it thrills me!
78. Wherever Kṛṣṇa, the lord of yoga, is, and wherever Arjuna the archer is, there also will be good fortune, and victory, and prosperity, and steadfast guidance. This I know!

Notes

One

1. The opening narrative of the Bhagavad Gītā is presented from the point of view of the rivals, the cousins, of our epic's heroes, the Pāṇḍavas. The first person quoted in the Bhagavad Gītā is the story's major villain, Duryodhana, whose very name, "One Difficult to Defeat," also has clear connotations of "the Cheater," which in fact he was. The Bhagavad Gītā alludes to cheating gamblers in dice games at 10.36, a clear reference to Duryodhana, who cheats in a dice game with his cousins.
2. In this *śloka* I have followed the emendation suggested by van Buitenen in Ludo Rocher (ed.), *Studies in Indian Literature and Philosophy* (Delhi: Motilal Banarsidass, 1988), which switches the order of the two names Bhīṣma and Bhīma. The critical edition has them in the opposite order, which makes no sense: Bhīṣma is a Kaurava opposed to Arjuna and the Pāṇḍavas, whereas Bhīma is one of the Pāṇḍava brothers! There is some dispute about other words in this stanza, but I think that this emendation is the best solution.

3. The word *dharma* occurs three times in this *śloka*: first in the compound *kuladharma* (traditional laws of the family), then *dharma* (traditional law), and finally *adharma* (lawlessness or chaos). Here and in the following stanzas, the "collapse of social order" refers to the mixing of castes.

Two

1. "The embodied one": this translates the Sanskrit term *dehin*, discussed briefly in the Introduction. The relation between the body (*deha*) and the embodied one (*dehin*, also *śarīrin*) is the same as that between the body (*deha*, also *śarīra*) and the soul or self (*ātman*). Just as the *ātman* resides in the body but is ultimately uncontaminated by contact with it, so too the *dehin*, "the embodied one," should not be confused with the body itself. The term *dehin* is basically a synonym for the eternal *ātman*.
2. Here the Sanskrit word for "embodied one" is *śarīrin*.
3. Here and in the following stanzas, the words mentioned above for the "embodied one," that is, the *ātman*, are conspicuously avoided. Instead we have the probably deliberately vague masculine pronouns "this one," "him," "he," etc.
4. Here finally, after several stanzas, we have explicit reference to "the embodied one": *dehin*.
5. That is, the "embodied one," though none of the Sanskrit words for this notion is used here. Instead we have a string of pronouns.
6. The Sanskrit term here is *dehin*.
7. The Sanskrit term for "your own caste duties" is *svadharma*, "one's own *dharma*."
8. That is, a war of *dharma*.
9. "Insight": the Sanskrit word here is *buddhi*, a very important term in the Bhagavad Gītā.

10. "Practice of yoga": this phrase translates the word *dharma*, here in the sense "practice." The word *yoga* doesn't occur here but is implied by the previous *śloka*, where it is explicit.
11. That is, *buddhi.*
12. "Intense concentration" translates the important yogic term *samādhi*, here as well as in stanzas 53 and 54.
13. "Remain within the self": more literally "be possessed of the *ātman*."
14. This is a very emphatic rejection of "all of the Vedas" (*sarveṣu vedeṣu*).
15. Here and elsewhere in this translation, the Sanskrit word for the high-caste priest, the Brahmin, is *brāhmaṇa*. See note 18 and, in Chapter 4, note 5.
16. The word *ātman* is used a second time here, perhaps with a double meaning: "himself" and "the self."
17. In this famous *śloka* the yogin is portrayed as hard at work on self-control while others sleep, whereas when others are hard at work on their various worldly pursuits, he sleeps.
18. "The sublime peace of Brahman": in Sanskrit this is *brahmanirvāṇa*, that is, the *nirvāṇa* of Brahman. This strange expression combines a fundamentally Hindu term for the absolute (*brahman*) with a fundamentally Buddhist term for ultimate peace (*nirvāṇa*). It seems to suggest that Hindu (that is, Brahma) *nirvāṇa* is greater than Buddhist *nirvāṇa*. If so, it is a cleverly understated rebuke "to whom it may concern": that is, to Buddhists.

Three

1. In this stanza the yoga of knowledge (*jñānayoga*) is contrasted with the yoga of action (*karmayoga*). Much of this chapter is devoted to a discussion of action, or *karman.*

2. Prajāpati is a late Vedic god whose name literally means "the lord of progeny" or "the lord of descendants." The Sanskrit word *prajā* and the English word *progeny* are related to each other etymologically, having the same linguistic origins.
3. Parjanya is the god of rain.
4. The word *akṣara,* which occurs here in the middle of the long compound *brahmākṣarasamudbhavam,* has two senses: "imperishable" and the sacred syllable *OM.*
5. In this stanza there is emphatic repetition of the word *ātman.*
6. "Work": that is, action (*karman*).
7. "The three conditions of nature": *prakṛteḥ guṇaiḥ.* Here and in the following *śloka*s, there is a brief discussion of the *guṇa*s, "conditions," and of *prakṛti,* "nature."
8. The Sanskrit word here is *manda.* It can mean "slow, sluggish, weak, dull, or stupid."
9. "One's own duty": *svadharma.*
10. "The condition of passion": that is, the second of the three *guṇa*s, or *raja*s (discussed in the Introduction).

Four

1. The Sanskrit word translated here as "power" is *māyā,* which has connotations of magical or supernatural power.
2. Duty is *dharma*; chaos is its opposite, *adharma.*
3. The adverb *sarvaśas* is ambiguous. Literally, it means "altogether, in all ways, wholly, completely, universally."
4. R. C. Zaehner, in *The Bhagavad Gītā* (London: Oxford University Press, 1969), translated this passage differently: "he only does such work as is needed for his body's maintenance."
5. Here and in general I have left the very important term *brahman* untranslated, but in order to give a sense of its significance, I have frequently added an adjective that is not in the Sanskrit

text: thus "infinite Brahman." This is justified by the fact that *brahman* elsewhere in the Bhagavad Gītā is modified by terms like *para* and *parama*, "supreme" (10.12) and *sanātana*, "eternal" (4.31). The term *brahman* is a neuter noun representing a cosmic principle, as opposed to the noun *brahman/brahmā*, which is masculine. Virtually all of the references to *brahman* in the Bhagavad Gītā are to the neuter noun, the only two exceptions coming in the crucial Chapter 11 (11.15 and 11.37). On this complex set of related words, see notes 15 and 18 to Chapter 2.

6. In this and in the following *ślokas* the literal offering of oblations into the sacrificial fire is compared with various sorts of symbolic sacrifices. This reflects the Bhagavad Gītā's interest in converting traditional Vedic sacrifice (which requires the killing of a sacrificial animal) into a symbolic or spiritual "sacrifice" (which requires no killing at all).
7. "Breath control": *prāṇayāma*.
8. "Cosmic breaths": of Brahman.
9. "The sacrifice of knowledge" probably means a sacrifice that is performed with knowledge and understanding. It may also mean that the pursuit of knowledge and understanding is a form of sacrifice.

Five

1. "Renunciation": the Sanskrit term here is *saṁnyāsa*. This is a key term in the Bhagavad Gītā, as is the related term *saṁnyāsin*. A *saṁnyāsin* is a person who has renounced his caste duties and social obligations, either withdrawing into a monastic tradition or leading the life of a wandering possessionless mendicant. I have chosen to leave this term untranslated on occasion in order to call attention to its importance among practitioners of yoga. On the other hand, I have translated *saṁnyāsa* consistently as "renunciation," as most translators do. See the useful overview by

Patrick Olivelle, "The Renouncer Tradition," in Gavin Flood, ed., *The Blackwell Companion to Hinduism* (Oxford: Blackwell, 2003).

2. Here as elsewhere, the term *ātman* can be translated as "the self" or "himself"or "his self."
3. The compound *brahmayoga* is itself part of a long four-word compound, *brahmayoga-yukt'ātmā* which can be analyzed in a number of ways. Some translators prefer to interpret it as "his self is joined or yoked to Brahman by means of yoga." Like Franklin Edgerton, I prefer to take the compound *brahmayoga* as a unit and interpret it to mean a type of yoga that is devoted to Brahman. Note the similar compound in stanzas 24–26 immediately following: *brahmanirvāṇa,* "the sublime peace of Brahman." This compound, which also occurs in the last stanza of Chapter 2, seems to be a clever attempt to assimilate the term *nirvāṇa,* a fundamental term in Buddhism, to Brahman, which is a fundamental term of Hinduism.

Six

1. The opening stanza reiterates what was said above at the opening of Chapter 5 (see that chapter's note 1). In this stanza van Buitenen sees an allusion to "Buddhists and other unorthodox who reject Vedic ritual." *Bhagavad Gītā,* p. 165.
2. There is a double meaning here. The word *āsana* means both "seat" and "yogic posture."
3. The phrase *śānti nirvāṇaparama* is usually understood to mean "the peace that culminates in *nirvāṇa,*" as I have translated it here, but I agree with van Buitenen that it may well suggest "the peace that is beyond *nirvāṇa,*" in which case it is an expression of anti-Buddhist sentiment.

4. In light of the previous note, it may not be far-fetched to see an allusion to Jainism in the phrase "nor for someone who refuses to eat at all."
5. "Devotes himself to me": the Sanskrit verb here is *bhajate*, from the verbal root *bhaj-*. It is the same root from which the term *bhakti* is derived. This stanza thus implicitly asserts that *bhakti* devotionalism is the highest form of yoga.

Seven

1. What follows is a brief discussion of the three *guṇas*.
2. *Guṇa* is here translated as "strand" instead of "condition," in order to reinforce the stanza's weaving metaphor.
3. To reinforce the emphasis on delusion here, the poet repeats the word *moha*: *saṁmoham*, "complete delusion," and *dvandva-moha*, "deluded by dualism" (which is repeated in the next stanza).

Eight

1. This chapter initiates a discussion of a set of traditional terms going back to the Upaniṣads: *adhyātma*, "that which has to do with the *ātman*"; *adhibhūta*, "that which has to do with beings in general"; and *adhidaiva* (also *adhidaivata*), "that which has to do with the world of the gods."
2. In this stanza a fourth term is added to the set: *adhiyajña*, "that which has to do with sacrifice." The Gītā uses this technical Vedic vocabulary with great familiarity and ease. A good discussion of these terms appears in Zaehner, *The Bhagavad Gītā* pp. 259–61.
3. "The individual spirit": the Sanskrit term is *puruṣa*.

4. The syllable *OM* has been sacred to Hindus going all the way back to the earliest Vedas. It has been referred to in the Gītā already at 3.15. Here it initiates the stanza, just as it initiates and closes traditional Vedic recitations. At 9.17, in a long series of "I am . . ." assertions, Kṛṣṇa identifies himself as this sacred syllable. At 17.23–24 *OM* is identified once again with infinite Brahman.
5. Kṛṣṇa identifies himself with the eternal unmanifest state. But the pronouns here are masculine, and it would seem that Kṛṣṇa is referring to himself, perhaps by pointing to himself as he speaks these words.

Nine

1. Here and in the following stanzas there is a discussion of "nature," in Sanskrit *prakṛti*.
2. Here as at 8.20, Kṛṣṇa seems to point to himself.
3. *Soma* is the celebrated Vedic drink of immortality. It was also the name of the plant from which the drink, a juice, was extracted. Soma was also much celebrated as a god. There has been much discussion about the nature of this drink and many attempts to identify the plant, but no general consensus has emerged. For details, see George Thompson, "On the Nāmarūpa of Soma," *Nāmarūpa: Categories of Indian Thought*, no. 5 (Fall 2006–Spring 2007).
4. There is wordplay here: *yogakṣema* in this instance means "success and peace," but also implies "yoga and peace."

Ten

1. Power, or manifestation (Sanskrit *vibhūti*) is discussed in the Introduction. This is a central term in this chapter, the only one in which it occurs.
2. As noted in the Introduction, the name Śiva never occurs in the Bhagavad Gītā. Instead Śiva is referred to here by a euphemistic epithet: Śaṁkara, the Gentle One.
3. The Sanskrit name for this cow is *kāmaduh*, mentioned also at 3.10. Note the word *kāma*, "desire" and often "erotic desire."
4. This is the only stanza where the name Rāma occurs. It is generally taken to be a reference to Rāma as an avatar of Viṣṇu, but it is striking that Rāma is mentioned only as the best "among men bearing arms." This is not strong evidence that Rāma was considered an avatar of Viṣṇu in the Bhagavad Gītā.
5. The Sanskrit word here is *dvandva*, literally "the pair, the two," as for example in the English compound "mother-and-father."
6. Alternatively, one could translate this phrase as "feminine qualities or powers."

Eleven

1. In order to see Kṛṣṇa as he really is, to see his "majestic [or "royal"] yoga" (*yogam aiśvaram*), Arjuna first must receive divine eyesight. In the next stanza the Gītā's "omniscient narrator," Saṁjaya, describes what Arjuna sees as Kṛṣṇa's "supreme majestic form" (*paramaṁ rūpam aiśvaram).*
2. Here Viṣṇu is referred to by one of his many epithets: Hari.
3. This is one of the rare instances in the Bhagavad Gītā where Kṛṣṇa is directly addressed as Viṣṇu.

4. This passage is high praise from Arjuna: it explicitly subordinates one of the three high gods of later Hinduism, Brahmā, to Kṛṣṇa. On this name see note 5 to Chapter 4.
5. On the iconography of Kṛṣṇa's four arms, which represent his four attributes (lotus, conch, discus, and mace), see Danielou, *Hindu Polytheism.*

Thirteen

1. "It has no qualities . . .": the term used here is *nirguṇa,* "without *guṇa*s." The term *guṇa* is central in this chapter.
2. "Material nature" is *prakṛti*; "the spirit in man" is *puruṣa.*

Fourteen

1. This chapter is largely devoted to an explanation of the three *guṇa*s: *sattva* (clarity), *rajas* (passion), and *tamas* (darkness). This last term, literally "darkness," strongly suggests "inertia" not only in the sphere of natural physics, but also in human psychology: sloth, sluggishness.

Fifteen

1. Here the Bhagavad Gītā clearly reveals its disdain for the Vedas. In other passages Kṛṣṇa is more inclined to accept the Vedas if they are offered to him as a sacrifice, or if they are performed as required by *dharma,* without any interest in the fruits.
2. *Vedānta* literally means "the culmination of the Vedas." In classical India it is the name of a school of philosophy that is most strongly associated with the philosopher Śaṁkara, a proponent of Advaita Vedānta, a philosophy of "nondualism" (Sanskrit, *advaita*) that recognized the ultimate religious authority of the

Vedas. Here, however, the term refers to the Upaniṣads, the latest texts of the Vedic tradition, which had an enormous influence on the Bhagavad Gītā. This subject is discussed in the Introduction.

Sixteen

1. This is possibly an allusion to Buddhism, which emphasizes desire as the cause of suffering. See the discussion of Buddhism, and its Four Noble Truths, in the Introduction.
2. "Lost souls": that is, lost *ātman*s. This stanza and the next seem to refer not to Buddhists and others like them, but rather to materialists, cynics, or hedonists.
3. This stanza and the next deal with the traditional Sanskrit texts that codify proper conduct in all walks of life. The Sanskrit word is *śāstra* (also attested at 17.1). Here, since the topic is karma, the reference is to texts that are known as *dharmaśāstra*s, that is, traditional lore, texts, or books devoted to the rules of *dharma*, or law. Other traditional *śāstra*s are devoted to nonreligious matters—for example, to the rules of conduct in the sphere of politics (*arthaśāstra*s) and even to the sphere of sex (*kāmaśāstra*s).

Seventeen

1. Literally, "OM that is the real."

Eighteen

1. Renunciation and abandonment: the Sanskrit terms are *saṁnyāsa* and *tyāga*. In general, they are synonyms (see *śloka*s 12.12 and 16.2, where *tyāga* is translated respectively as "abandonment" and "renunciation"). In this chapter, however, much care is given to distinguishing the two terms.

2. That is, physically, verbally, or mentally.
3. "Lawlessness": the Sanskrit is *adharma.*
4. "Renunciation": the Sanskrit is *saṁnyāsa.*
5. "By my grace": the Sanskrit is *matprasādāt.* In what follows there is much talk of Kṛṣṇa's "grace," that is, his *prasāda.*

Selected Bibliography

For those who would like to pursue further study of the Bhagavad Gītā, the following books and articles may be useful.

Scholarly Translations with Sanskrit Text and Elaborate Commentary

Franklin Edgerton, *The Bhagavad Gītā, Translated and Interpreted*, 2 volumes. Harvard Oriental Series. Cambridge, Mass.: Harvard University Press, 1946.

R. C. Zaehner, *The Bhagavad Gītā, with a Commentary Based on the Original Sources.* London: Oxford University Press, 1969.

J.A.B. van Buitenen, *The Bhagavad Gītā in the Mahābhārata: A Bilingual Edition, Text and Translation.* Chicago: University of Chicago Press, 1981.

Edgerton's translation is extremely literal, which makes it virtually unreadable. But it serves as a good, reliable analysis of the Sanskrit text for students. Zaehner's text is also unreadably dense for the general student, but for serious students of Hinduism and of the Sanskrit, it is very useful, with a very detailed commentary based on native commentaries. Van Buitenen's edition is unique because it gives both the Sanskrit and the English texts of the full section of the Mahābhārata in which the Bhagavad Gītā appears. It has a useful introduction and notes that have wisely been kept to a minimum.

See also Ludo Rocher, ed., *Studies in Indian Literature and Philosophy: Collected Articles of J.A.B. van Buitenen* (Delhi: Motilal Banarsidass, 1988). This collection contains many important articles, in particular "A Contribution to the Critical Edition of the Bhagavadgītā."

General Introductions to Hinduism

J. L. Brockington, *The Sacred Thread: Hinduism in its Continuity and Diversity*, 1981; repr., Edinburgh: University Press of Edinburgh, 1996.

Gavin Flood, *An Introduction to Hinduism.* Cambridge: Cambridge University Press, 1996.

Gavin Flood, ed., *The Blackwell Companion to Hinduism.* Oxford: Blackwell, 2003. This book consists of an introduction and twenty-seven essays by leading scholars that present the current scholarship on a wide range of issues, including Sanskrit textual traditions, regional traditions, major historical developments, and traditions of science, medicine, philosophy, and theology. It also features several essays on contemporary society and politics in India.

Axel Michaels, *Hinduism Past and Present.* Princeton, N.J.: Princeton University Press, 2004.

On Yoga

M. Eliade, *Yoga: Immortality and Freedom.* Bollingen Series. Princeton, N.J.: Princeton University Press, 1958.

Jean Varenne, *Yoga and the Hindu Tradition.* Chicago: University of Chicago Press, 1976.

There have been many translations of the *Yoga Sūtras* of Patañjali. A reliable scholarly one, but now out of date, is J. H. Woods, *The Yoga System of Patañjali.* Edwin Bryant of Rutgers University is presently making a new translation, which should soon be published.

Translations of the Mahābhārata and the Rāmāyaṇa

The complete scholarly translation of the Mahābhārata, sponsored by the University of Chicago, has not yet been completed. Van Buitenen translated the first five books before he died. The project has been resumed by James Fitzgerald, and other volumes are forthcoming.

The Rāmāyaṇa, not so vast as the Mahābhārata, is much closer to completion. Princeton University Press has published five of the seven projected volumes, under the direction of Robert Goldman.

The recently initiated Clay Sanskrit Library, in collaboration with New York University Press (JJC Foundation), is producing bilingual editions of many classical Sanskrit texts. They are modeled on the famous Loeb editions, published by Harvard University Press, of classical Greek and Latin authors. Many more editions are forthcoming.

A brief, nicely written one-volume synopsis of the Mahābhārata is William Buck, *Mahabharata Retold* (Berkeley and Los Angeles: University of California Press, 1973). Buck also produced a short one-volume summary of the Rāmāyaṇa: *The Ramayana Retold* (Berkeley and Los Angeles: University of California Press, 1981).

Though not at all scholarly, these books retell these epic tales with vigor and sensitivity.

Related Topics

On Epic Sanskrit, see John Brockington, "The Sanskrit Epics," in *Blackwell Companion.* For greater depth, see his *The Sanskrit Epics* (Leiden: Brill, 1998).

A brief but good collection of essays on the Bhagavad Gītā is Julius Lipner, ed., *The Fruits of Our Desiring: An Enquiry into the Ethics of the Bhagavadgītā for Our Times* (Calgary: Bayeux Arts, 1997).

On other epic traditions in India, including many contemporary ones, see S. Blackburn, P. Claus, J. Flueckiger, and S. Wadley, *Oral Epics in India* (Berkeley and Los Angeles: University of California Press, 1989).

On the important collection of Vedic dialogues and reflections, the Upaniṣads, see two recent translations:

Patrick Olivelle, *Upaniṣads, Translated from the Original Sanskrit.* Oxford: Oxford University Press, 1996.

Valerie Roebuck, *The Upaniṣads.* London and New York: Penguin Books, 2003.

On the notion that the author of the Bhagavad Gītā impersonates both Arjuna and Kṛṣṇa, see George Thompson, "Ahaṃkāra and Ātmastuti: Self-assertion and Impersonation in the Rigveda," *History of Religions* 37, no. 2 (1997), pp. 141–71. While this article is focused primarily on the Rigveda, it cites passages from the Bhagavad Gītā and the Upaniṣads and quotes examples of this genre from other world traditions.

Two companion volumes attempt to capture the influence of the Bhagavad Gītā on subsequent audiences. One is Eric Sharpe, *The Universal Gītā: Western Images of the Bhagavad Gītā: A Bicentenary Survey* (La Salle, Ill.: Open Court, 1985). It gives a useful sketch of the response in the West to the Bhagavad Gītā from 1785 to 1985 and contains brief discussions of the Bhagavad Gītā's influence on Gandhi, as well as on the American Transcendentalists Emerson and Thoreau and the poet T. S. Eliot. Sharpe also discusses its influence on Western occultism (e.g., Theosophy) and the American and European counterculture. The other companion volume is Arvind Sharma, *The Hindu Gītā: Ancient and Classical Interpretations of the Bhagavadgītā* (La Salle, Ill.: Open Court, 1986). This useful survey of the influence of the Bhagavad Gītā on subsequent Hinduism provides a valuable outline of the classical commentaries made by such influential figures as Bhāskara, Śaṁkara, Rāmānuja, and Madhva.

On Gandhi's reflections on the Bhagavad Gītā , see M. K. Gandhi, *MK Gandhi Interprets the Bhagavadgita* (Delhi: Orient Paperbacks, n.d.).

J. Robert Oppenheimer's quotation of the Bhagavad Gītā, and his subsequent ambivalance concerning his role in the development of the atomic bomb, are discussed in Roger Shattuck, *Forbidden Knowledge: From Prometheus to Pornography* (New York: St. Martin's Press, 1996).

On the Hindu triad of supreme gods, the Trimūrti, see A. Danielou, *Hindu Polytheism* (New York: Pantheon, 1964), which gives ample description of these three main gods of classical Hinduism: Brahmā, Viṣṇu, and Śiva. Besides citing the relevant textual sources, this book provides a wealth of illustrations of the iconography of these gods. There is also a useful discussion of the avatars of Viṣṇu.

On Buddhism in general, see H. Bechert and R. Gombrich, *The World of Buddhism: Buddhist Monks and Nuns in Society and Culture* (London: Thames & Hudson, 1984). This collection of essays by leading scholars covers the entire Buddhist world. Each essay provides a good overview of its subject.

A well-informed and accessible introduction to Jainism is offered by Paul Dundas, *The Jains*, 2nd ed. (1992; repr., London and New York: Routledge, 2002).

On magical thinking, see Joan Didion, *The Year of Magical Thinking* (New York: Alfred A. Knopf, 2005). On magical thinking in Vedic, see George Thompson, "On the Logic of Sacrifice in Vedic," a paper presented at the New England Conference of the Association for Asian Studies, at the University of Massachusetts Dartmouth, 2006.

Acknowledgments

I would like to thank my editor, Jeff Seroy—always perceptive, flexible, and patient—and his colleagues at Farrar, Straus and Giroux, for the great efforts they have made to help me to improve this translation and to make the Introduction more accessible. I also wish to thank Luis Gonzalez-Reimann, Anna Dallapiccola, Robert Moses and Eddie Stern, Stephanie Rutt, my students at Montserrat College of Art, and my friends at the Toadstool Bookshop in Peterborough, New Hampshire, all of whom have offered support and encouragement in so many ways. And last but not least, special thanks to Susan Prince Thompson, my best critic and my muse.